**PRESENTS**

Marijuana Success Volume 2

Ed Rosenthal

Quick American

Marijuana Success Volume 2
Copyright 2005 Ed Rosenthal

Project Editor: S Newhart
Typesetting and Cover Design: Scott Idleman/Blink
All articles and photos are © Ed Rosenthal unless otherwise credited.
Printed in China.

Quick American
A division of Quick Trading Company
Oakland, California
www.quicktrading.com

ISBN10: 0-932551-73-4
ISBN13: 978-0932-55173-3

Contents

INTRODUCTION

Marijuana Success Volume 2

First, I'd like to thank you for buying—or even considering purchasing—this volume. Whether your interest in this book is for the great marijuana photography or the creative and practical gardening tips, I think you will find that *Marijuana Success Volume 2* tickles the creative mind by presenting new ideas as well as visual candy for your enjoyment and use.

Growing a garden requires a mixture of practical know-how and intuitive sensibility. It is necessary to have a basic grasp on the elements that plants need to thrive, but a gardener also learns to read his or her plants and the signals they give.

In a lot of ways, growing a garden is like cooking. Most people can open a cookbook, follow the instructions, and produce some facsimile of the dish they set out to make. Likewise, nearly anyone can pick up a gardening manual, follow the botanical recipe of light, water and nutrients and grow a decent garden.

However when it comes to growing a truly great garden, just like making a gourmet quality meal, it requires a little something more. Connoisseurs are always looking for ways to improve the recipe, and they know how important it is to start with good quality ingredients.

Beyond this, much of the difference between producing something good and something great is in understanding the importance of nuance and being open to creative innovations.

Collected in these pages are essays that might open your eyes to new ways to make your garden great. This book is full of ideas and accounts of real gardens, indoors and out, that show you how gardeners have adapted their techniques to fit the situation.

In one article, a fellow is growing his own in a storage container that is sitting in his backyard. He has figured out how to modify his setup to produce a continuous harvest. Another essay was written with my old friend, Homer Grown. Homer is primarily an outdoor gardener who is always experimenting in different environments. In this account, he describes gardening in the desert—find out how he was able to bring in a crop in this inhospitable terrain. Another farmer decided to create a large indoor garden of medical-grade cannabis in California. He discusses his cultivation techniques and his garden setup in detail.

Not every garden is a complete success, but we can learn from others' mistakes. I take you into a garden that requires an "Extreme Garden Makeover" and show you how yield can be increased just by tweaking the garden

in some minor ways. First step, new curtains...

Many essays in *Marijuana Success Volume 2* describe creative methods that gardeners use to produce bountiful yields. The article on "Late Planting" shows you how gardeners can start an outdoor garden in mid–summer or later and still have good yields. "Outdoor Hydroponics" shows how real gardeners use soilless techniques under the sun. Finally "Growing in the Limits" offers tips for producing an optimal garden within the most common legal guidelines for medical grows.

Another set of articles offers solutions for common gardening concerns. "Camouflaged Gardens" shows various ways that growers protect the greenery from prying eyes. "Regeneration: The Third Way" describes how to re-flower the same plants over and over instead of starting each garden anew. An article on "Eco-Cultivation" considers the impact of marijuana gardeners on the environment, and makes suggestions for how to be as earth friendly as possible.

Finally, "Harvest Problem Solving" addresses bringing in the crop successfully. What do gardeners do when bad weather threatens plants that are almost ripe? This essay helps you make sense out of this and many other common harvest situations.

Two essays, "The Future of Marijuana Breeding" and "Gender Bending" explore techniques and new developments that can be applied when gardeners decide to venture into breeding. Learn how to make males, read about the progenitors of today's varieties and find out the trends for future variety developments.

After harvesting the buds, "Fresh Leaves, Fresh Hash" shows you how one gardener extends his harvest by making hash from the fresh, undried leaves. An hour after harvest the leaves have been converted to hash. Last but not least, I take you to see the actual creation of the "Hashimals." These carbon-based creatures have been proven to bring joy wherever they go. This article shows you how they are made, how to recognize them and how to care for them.

Marijuana Success Volume 2 presents more than information, it presents innovation. Here you will find advice that extends what you've learned in grow books. You will see the successes, failures and solutions that real gardeners bring to critical problems.

Grow books present general information that can guide you in the right direction. The gardens shown here have modified that information to fit real-life situations. By looking at how they have designed and cultivated great crops in real environments, this book shows the practical side of nuance.

Great gardens, like great cooking, often come from people who have cultivated a passionate interest in their subject matter. A gardener may have a naturally intuitive "green thumb" or a more in-depth scientific understanding of the botanical processes in play. Whether guided more by the art or the science of growing, their success almost always includes a passionate connection to their subject matter.

With that in mind, this book was designed to motivate you with the beauty of this plant in its different guises. You are sure to find beautiful gardens, beautiful plants and beautiful buds in these pages.

Beauty is important because it soothes the mind and at the same time, it provokes the wildest fantasies. The visions and thoughts that it inspires are also what this book is about. Marijuana often serves as a tool and guide to a greater recognition of beauty, an appreciation of new ideas and novel approaches, and of course, sometimes to an appreciation of snacks.

Seriously though, *Marijuana Success Volume 2* is ultimately about creative gardening, and I invite you to join in and expand your own toolbox for innovation in the garden. My hope is that this book will help you envision success in your adventures with gardening marijuana, an herb whose very design is meant to help us envision.

GROWING THE

This garden was used to produce medical-grade marijuana. The principal grower was an experienced hand and was interested in producing a high yield of the best quality medicine. The room was designed for ease of production and efficiency. The beauty of the garden was evidence of the care the growers put into it.

KIND INDOORS
home gardening

EARLY IN THEIR TRIALS, they found that one of the easiest ways to improve the quality of yield was by pruning the plants so they produce fewer, but much bigger buds. The size of the plants, the targeted plant size at harvest and each plant's natural shape should determine the type and style of the trim. Recently I observed a garden in which different trimming techniques were used depending on when the plants were placed into flowering.

The gardeners came to the realization that both they and the plants did best for their gardening style when the plants were pruned to four branches, or leads, per square foot. This formula did not change no matter the size the plants were grown to, the size of the containers or the growing method used.

The garden was filled with 10-inch black containers in two trays. One tray held forty-four containers in eleven rows lined four deep, side-to-side. The grow space was lit by four 600-watt horizontal high-pressure sodium (HPS) lamps. The 4' x 10' area was lined with white polyethylene plastic on three sides and Styrofoam boards, which were easily moved around, on the fourth.

The other tray held fifty-two containers in thirteen rows, four deep. It was lit by five 600-watt HPS lamps, and was also surrounded by polyethylene and Styrofoam reflectors.

> **"...one of the easiest ways to improve the quality of yield is by pruning the plants so they produce fewer, but much bigger buds. "**

In a previous garden, plants were grown in square 6-inch pots. These plants were pruned to one lead so that four plants (and four buds) fit into a square foot. However, the buds didn't grow as large as when the plants were placed in 10-inch containers and trimmed to four leads. In a later garden, the size of the containers was increased to 12 inches and the bud size increased again. It appeared that the volume of planting mix affected bud size. The 10-inch container holds seven times the volume of planting mix of a 6-inch container. A 12-inch container holds one and a half times the volume of a 10-inch container. The gardeners concluded that plants with larger root systems support larger buds.

The planting mix was all-organic, consisting of 10% each peat moss and worm castings, and 40% each vermiculite and perlite. (Rather than using vermiculite, gardeners should use coir or peat moss, which is assured not to contain asbestos). Rock phosphate

Above: This plant in a 6" container was trimmed to a main stem and two side stems. The center bud would have grown larger without the two side branches. Below: Garden trimmed to six to eight leads yielded more total bud, but much of it was of lesser quality.

Plants in 6" containers. The group on the left has been pruned to a single lead. The ones on the right haven't been pruned yet.

was added to the mix at the rate of 1/2-tablespoon per container. At other times, the growers had used planting

> "The gardeners concluded that plants with larger root systems support larger buds."

mixes, and horticultural clay pellets. The plants were placed in the containers as rooted clones when they were about 6 inches high, with two or three sets of leaves. The original intent was to grow White Widow clones, in an area 4' x 10' lit by four 600-watt HPS lamps, vegetatively under constant light for about 10 days. In addition the Soma Jack clones would be ready for the five-light system. This consisted of a space 4' x 13'. It was lit by five 600-watt HPS lamps. It held 13 rows of 10-inch containers four deep. By the time

the plants would be placed into flowering, approximately 10 days after the Jacks were planted, the White Widows would be 18 to 24 inches tall.

That plan fell through for three reasons. First, the Jack clones were not

ready on time. Second, when the plants were ready, the gardeners were busy doing other things. Third, the gardeners found a great demand for the clones and decided to keep the plants in vegetative growth an extra 20 days while taking cuttings from the undergrowth. By the time they were forced to flower, the White Widows were in vegetative growth for a total of 40 days and the Jacks had 20 days of continuous light.

The White Widows were 3 feet tall when they were finally placed in flowering. By the time they were ripe, they had grown 3 1/2-foot long stems, which supported only the top canopy. The plants were 5 to 6 feet tall at ripening.

Plants in 10" containers. They were pruned to four leads. The yield of high quality bud was larger than when the plants were trimmed to six to eight leads. Each of the plant's four stems was supported by a single wooden or metal stake.

The plants were originally supported using bamboo stakes, but they grew too tall and heavy for them. The bamboo was replaced by either 6-foot long, 1-inch-square wooden stakes or 6-foot tall plastic-coated metal stakes. Both of these worked well for supporting the plants. The stakes were pushed to the bottom of the containers to keep them sturdy. Then the plants were tied to them using 8-inch paper coated twist ties found in nurseries.

The plants were pruned three times, at 10-to 15-day intervals before they were forced into flowering. Rather than cutting the tops, causing the plants to branch more, the lower growth was removed. At forcing and again about two weeks later, the plants were pruned, allowing only four main branches to remain on the plants. With the staking and removal of extraneous vegetation, each lead had direct access to light and adequate growing space.

The containers were fed by hand as needed, usually every 3 to 5 days. This was determined by feeling the planting mix in several containers 2 inches below the surface. If it "felt moist rather than dry," it was not watered. The growers figured that there was much more moisture in the bottom third of the container than in the top. Only when the top of the container was dry, was the rest of the container ready to be watered.

To start the watering process, a 30-gallon plastic trashcan was filled with nutrient-water mix. A 5-gallon container was dipped into the can and filled with the mix and then pulled out. This made a convenient portable reservoir. Watering was accomplished using a 2-quart water pitcher. It was dipped into the 5-gallon bucket of water-nutrient solution for filling. The water was poured from the pitcher directly into the plant container. The pitcher was a convenient measure because it assured that all the containers were irrigated equally and provided enough water so the containers drained a bit, flushing out excess salts.

The lights were evenly spaced through each garden, averaging 60 watts input per square foot for the White Widow tray and 57.7 watts psf for the Jacks. The horizontal HPS lamps were screwed into Hydrofarm reflectors, which are reported to be very efficient. The lamps were attached to the 11-foot ceilings using a hook screwed into a 2" x 4" board bolted to the ceiling using mollies. The lamps had a V holder on either side ending in an S hook. The S hooks on either side of the lamp were moved up or down the chain to raise or lower the light.

The reflectors were stationary, but with the close spacing of the lamps and the 2-foot distance between the top of the canopy and the bottom of the lamps, light from the lamps crossed quite a bit. Also, any light that hit the white Styrofoam or polyethylene plastic was reflected back to the garden. The evenly spaced leads had enough room between them for light to penetrate a foot or more down from the top of the canopy.

The reflectors were ventilated and were outfitted with fans to prevent heat build-up in the room. This lowered the temperature in the room significantly so less air conditioning was required. The nine-light ballasts were kept in a separate space—a closet that had a small vent fan which removed the ballast heat to the attic.

A CO2 generator supplemented the room with higher CO2 content. It was kept at 1600 PPM using an online meter connected directly to the generator. The generator created a lot of heat and some moisture in the room. A humidistat set at 60% humidity drew out the excess humidity.

Ripe Soma Jack bud. Crystals cover the vegetation. The male flower (left middle) appears at maturity so it does no damage. However the pollen is viable and can be used for seedmaking.

With the nine lights and a CO2 generator going, a lot of heat was created: 3,200 BTUs per 1000 watts. There was about 5,400 watts plus heat from the burning natural gas CO2 generator. About 18,800 BTUs were created by the lights and perhaps 3,200 by the generator. Without air conditioning and ventilation, the temperature would quickly rise to 90-100 degrees F on a 70-degree day. On a 90-degree day, the room temperature would climb to 110 degrees F.

To prevent this extreme heat scenario, the room was cooled using an external air conditioner, which supplied cool air from a vent in the wall near the ceiling. The air-cooled reflectors removed close to half the heat before it entered the room. Rather than using high-powered ventilation or air conditioning, two 6-inch inline fans moved the heat generated by the light bulbs.

Air circulation was provided by a ceiling fan and several window fans mounted near the ceiling. In addition two turbo fans placed close to each other on the floor blew air up to the ceiling.

The Soma Jacks in the larger tray had a different experience than their neighbors across the aisle. They had been placed into the garden 20 days later and received only two "haircuts," one at forcing and the other three weeks into flowering. They were only 15 to 18 inches tall at flowering and matured at less than 3 feet.

At the first trimming, plants were reduced to 3 to 5 leads. They were staked and tied to hold the leads in position. The second trim, which took place between flowering weeks 2 and 3, removed branches that had grown since forcing.

The trim was used as cuttings for cloning. They were placed back into a vegetative garden and took an extra three weeks to revert from flowering to vegetative growth. They were not ready to plant until five weeks after cutting.

Three weeks after forcing, new branch growth tapered off. The plants put all of their energy into reproduction, producing clusters of flowers all along the branches. The clusters often link up, forming a solid "bud" consisting of the female flowers' stigmas, to which any floating pollen adheres. Since these plants were all female, there was no stray pollen so all of the flowers remained unpollinated, that is, sinsemilla.

The pruning given to these plants at forcing and 2 or 3 weeks later is similar to the ones wine grape vines or fruit trees undergo. All branches extraneous to the gardeners' plant needs are removed. Before the final pruning a plant might have 16 or 20 branches. The top four are usually the strongest and have the most development. The rest are usually much smaller.

After pruning, only 4 or 5 branches were left. The small under-canopy branches and buds were clipped along with less developed branches. Under-canopy buds are small, don't mature well and take energy from the upper canopy buds, which produce larger, tighter, more uniform maturing bud that is higher quality and easier to manicure.

The top buds weighed a little more than 8 pounds, a disappointing return. This was attributed to setting the CO_2 unit inaccurately and the air conditioning unit malfunctioning during the five-week period critical to bud development. Temperatures soared into the 90s for several days during the critical fifth week of flowering, halfway to ripening.

Although the yield was disappointing the potency and quality of the buds was superb.

White Widow bud. The stigmas are drying, the ovaries enlarging and the trichomes filling. The bud will be ready in about a week.

MORE THAN

You can tell a lot about a person by looking at their garden. Character is expressed in its construction and the care of the plants. It is only natural that this is so. The green room is part of one's life—and is treated in the same way as house care, dress or grooming.

ENOUGH
the continuous harvest

CARL IS A PERFECT EXAMPLE. He is a modest person, but totally independent. He lives in a set of converted structures in a poor neighborhood. His garden is not flashy but it produces more than enough high quality weed. He is enjoying life and has no expectations of a change in circumstances.

Carl has been growing his own for years and is always innovating. He is a medical user so he has easy access to the many clone varieties available at the dispensaries in San Francisco and Oakland. Currently he is growing BC Big Bud, Ice (which he described as a combination of White Widow and Big Bud), Black Domina and California Orange.

He has designed his medicinal garden to provide him with a continuous harvest. It is divided into three separate spaces: an area for clones, a vegetative room and a flowering room. Every week new plants are started and old ones are harvested.

Carl used to take his own clones, but now there are many varieties of high quality clones available, so he no longer bothers. Instead he picks out new varieties that intrigue him. The newly purchased clones are placed in a horticultural tray in rockwool under two full-spectrum fluorescent tubes.

> **"You can tell a lot about a person by looking at their garden. "**

Carl covers them with a dome for about ten days and waters them every day. After the dome is removed, they are planted in 3-inch containers using new planting mix. They stay in these containers under the fluorescents until there is space for them in the vegetative room. A cutting typically spends about ten days under cover and ten days in the 3-inch container under fluorescents.

Next, they are given space in the vegetative chamber, where they grow in the small pots for only two weeks. Then they are transplanted to 6-inch containers for a three-week stay. Finally, in their third and final transplant, they graduate to 12-inch-diameter containers.

The vegetative garden space is 4' x 5' and about 7 1/2 feet tall. It is lit by a

The vegetative garden. Plants start out in 3-inch containers and leave in 12-inch-diameter pots that will support them through flowering.

Finished bud going through the second stage of the curing/drying process. Below: A photo of the grow space before it was converted to a garden.

single 400-watt HPS moving on a track adjusted to 1 1/2 feet above the canopy. The light track evens out the light dispersion to the plants.

Carl waters the vegetative garden with nutrient solution using a turkey baster daily. The baster holds about three ounces of water. Each container receives three basters of water, which follows the label instructions for the General Hydroponics three-part mix for vegetative growth. The plants also get a capful of Earth Juice Catalyst per gallon of water. Carl doesn't use a ppm, EC or pH meter, but he does use a water meter to check on the moisture in the containers. Generally he waters more during the summer and less in the winter. There is no excess water flow from the containers.

During the time the plants are in the vegetative room, they grow from the small rooting cuttings to sturdy two-foot-tall plants. Ventilation in the space is provided by a 6-inch inline fan, which pulls out the hot spent air. "The fan is quiet and runs forever," he says. The fan is regulated by a thermostat set to turn on at 80 degrees F. The fan shuts off when the temperature gets down to 73 degrees F. A 4-inch flexible tube brings in fresh, cool outside air from underneath the structure. Except on the hottest days, the temperature in the garden stays below 80 degrees F.

Plants leave the vegetative garden

when space opens up in the flowering room. When the plants are first introduced to the room, they are placed along the walls, to the side of the light. As they get closer to finishing, they move toward the center.

The flower room is a space 7' x 7 1/2' and 7 1/2 feet high. It contains nearly fifty plants. It is lit by a single 1000-watt HPS lamp on a motorized track. The light travels two feet before it makes a return trip across the garden. The light is kept on twelve hours a day, leaving the plants with twelve hours of uninterrupted darkness each day.

The room is equipped with a 20-pound CO_2 tank that has an automated meter, which keeps the CO_2 level at 1000 parts per million. The tube from the CO_2 tank is attached to a rotating 12-inch table fan so the CO_2 circulates freely in the space. A 6-inch inline fan is used in the room as well, to remove the hot air that builds up in the garden. A thermostat also controls this room's fan, and draws in cool air from under the structure to replenish the garden. The temperature stays between 75 to 80 degrees F when the light is on and no lower than 60 degrees F when it is off.

All the plants in the flowering room are fertilized with General Hydro "Flora" brand 3-part mix configured for bloom.

The plants are kept on the dry side and are given a major watering only once a week. They are given a sprinkle daily. Carl's purpose in limiting water is to control height. However, this may be costing him significant yield. He plans to try supplying more water to a few of the plants and see if there is an increase in yield.

When Carl was growing his own starter plants, the varieties were consistent in their ripening time. Each week, four or five plants would mature. Now that he is trying new varieties, it isn't as regular as it used to be, because the ripening time for each variety is a little different.

Each plant is harvested in three stages over a week. First, the top buds are removed. This opens the middle and lower buds to the light. In three to four days, the middle buds are ready for harvest. The lower buds are given their chance in the sun and are harvested after another three or four days. Then the container is removed from the garden. The soil is used in the outdoor garden for landscaping, and the containers are thoroughly washed with anti-bacterial soap and then re-used.

The remaining plants are moved around so that the most mature get the choice spots under the lamp and

Left: All of the controls are placed on a shelf, above the water line. The rotating circulation fan also distributes CO_2 from the tank kept below. The plastic tube in front of the fan emits the CO_2 and it is blown into the garden area. Top: A BC Big Bud in vegetative growth. This plant is going into the flowering room within a week.

the newly introduced plants are on the periphery. Before the new ones move to the flowering garden, each plant is given a little pruning.

The buds are trimmed and then hung to dry in a cool dark spot with a mild draft. When they are just getting the least bit crispy, they are placed on a small window screen and turned a few times a day. They cure into high quality hard nugs that are a pleasure to smoke. All the bud varieties are labeled and kept separately.

When Carl was still cutting his own starter plants, he took about three cuttings from each plant for the next generation. Only one of them was likely to make it into the garden. The extra cuttings provided flexibility in choosing plants. For instance, if a variety that he tested was a winner, the three cuttings allowed him to increase its population. Now he obtains clones at the dispensaries.

Spider mites were the only pest that used to plague the garden. Pyrethrum bombs were used to keep the pests under control, but the mites had developed a bit of immunity to it, and the powerful aerosol burned the leaves. About a month ago, Carl started to spray with neem oil on a weekly basis. The mites have disappeared and the leaves have a nice glossy look. The neem oil gums up the mites' proboscces, resulting in their starvation.

The clone area. These plants are waiting for space to open up in the vegetative garden. They are growing under two 4-foot long 40-watt cool white fluorescents. The heat mat keeps the trays of clones at about 72 degrees F.

A virulent race of powdery mildew plagues San Francisco Bay Area grow rooms and is also present in many other areas of North America and Europe. It has never been a problem in this garden, but some of the starter plants he purchased were infected with it. He clipped off the worst leaves and used the neem oil. The mildew disappeared.

Neem oil also acts as a prophylactic against infection. One of the ways neem oil protects is the physical barrier that the oil creates. Mold spores cannot contact the docking area on the leaf that they need to connect to in order to start growing. It is also dis-

tasteful and gumming to many insects. Carl's system is simple and elegant. He staggers the plants' growing phases, so that they are at different levels of maturation depending on when they were introduced. Rotating plants on a weekly basis allows him

Top: Typical bud from the BC Big Bud strain.

Varieties:

BC BIG BUD- This indica has a lot of consistency. It comes in all the time and is easy to grow. It stays compact so I can pack the plants in. Its taste is great and I like the high.

ICE- is a cross of Big Bud and White Widow. This is the first time I'm growing it. It's too big for this garden and spreads its branches too much. It's probably better as an outdoor plant.

BLACK DOMINA- This plant spreads to about an 18-inch diameter in a 12-inch container if it's not topped. When it's topped it spreads out to two feet or more. It has a unique high and I find it has great healing properties.

Future Plans:

"I am building a 4' x 4' finishing room. It will be all bright white and will hold only 8 to 12 plants during the last month of flowering. This way I can give the maturing plants special treatment. I'm also planning on adding a 400-watt HPS in the flowering room. The plants coming in from the vegetative room would be placed directly under the 400, although they would also get side light from a 1000. The older plants would be more directly under the 1000. They will move into the 4' x 4' room during the last two or three weeks."

to harvest continuously and perpetually. In addition to staggering the introduction of new plants, Carl also controls growth by restricting light and water, giving the prime care to the plants closest to harvest.

Every week, Carl harvests two to four ounces of personal stash. For a while, he was only growing one variety, BC Big Bud, not only because of its enjoyable high, but also because of its hardiness and very consistent flowering time. Now that he is more experienced

with maintaining a continuous harvest, he has introduced other varieties into the garden. Ripening times differ by variety, which makes timing a little more complex, but allows Carl to diversify his stash to include a few different flavors and effects.

ECO-CULTIVATION

Jack Herer, the author of *The Emperor Wears No Clothes*, claims that marijuana was criminalized in order to prohibit hemp cultivation. This was the government's first anti-ecological policy regarding cannabis and its anti-marijuana strategies are creating more environmental havoc now than ever before.

environmental gardening

BECAUSE OF government pressure, growers have gone indoors, using electricity—rather than the sun—to illuminate their gardens. Every grower knows how injurious increased electric usage can be to one's finances. The bright lights have been a bonanza for utility companies and a devastating blow to the cause of conservation. In fact, California's recent energy crisis is in part a result of increased home cultivation and marijuana suppliers turning up the amps as a result of Prop. 215 (The California Medical Marijuana Law).

There are probably 50 million active tokers in the US. It's estimated that 10 percent of them, or 5 million people, grow their own using lights. Although some gardens are very small and use only a 1000 watts, some are considerably larger. Let's say they average 3000 watts, or three kilowatts.

During the vegetative part of the cycle, which takes about a month, the lights are on continuously; during flowering, about 10 weeks, they are on for only 12 hours a day. That averages out to about 16 hours, or 16 kilowatt-hours per light per day. An average garden uses about 50 kilowatts a day.

On a yearly basis a single light uses approximately 5694 kilowatt-hours. The average, three-light garden uses about 18,250 kilowatts a year just for lighting.

Multiply that by the estimated million indoor growers, and the total figure comes to 91.25 trillion kilowatt-hours.

This is only part of the ecological damage created as a result of anti-pot laws. When the back-to-the-land movement started in the late '60s, people had a philosophical commitment to the land. They rejected the sterile chemical-farming process in favor of a nurturing one; if the soil is fed, it will feed the plants.

In 1975 I met some organic growers who backpacked several tons of turkey manure up and down three miles of rough mountain trail to their hidden garden. These people felt they had a responsibility to the forest in which they grew, so they would not even consider the use of chemicals on the earth, which they considered sacred. They

didn't realize that forest plants were adapted to a light fertilization program. Adding all that nutrient to the forest ecology created a different ecological situation, favoring a different set of organisms.

After 35 years of skirmishes and wars, guerrilla growers have changed their philosophy. Instead of deploying tons of low-grade organic fertilizers, most contemporary guerrilla farmers use concentrated chemicals. A ton of 3-2-2 is the equivalent of 400 pounds of 15-10-10. Though most growers try to do as little damage as possible, pot patches usually disturb the ecology of the growing area. Both chemical and organic fertilizers upset the nutrient values of the soil. Herbicides and pesticides mess up natural checks and balances. Dedicating land to a wilderness garden limits its use by animals, and contradicts the intent of setting aside space for wilderness.

What can the indoor or outdoor grower do to minimize damage to the environment in an era of insane government policies? I think we have to use a cost-benefit analysis of the situation.

First, on a very practical level, intersection with the law is very anti-ecological. Vast amounts of paper are generated

This seedling patch was designed with the environment in mind. It was placed in a natural clearing in the forest and partially constructed with indigenous material that was returned to the forest after the seedlings were transplanted. They were grown in a medium made in reusable containers. Rather than using traps or poisons, barriers were employed to keep animals away.

and hundreds of hours of people's time is wasted—including cops', prosecutors', judges', defense attorneys' and defendants' time. This is one factor that must be taken into account when any other savings are considered.

Here are some things growers can do to minimize damage to the environment that results from cannabis prohibition.

Indoors

Lights use high levels of electricity. Electric power is generated by burning oil, coal or gas; using nuclear reactors to heat water and run turbines; or hydroelectrically, by damming rivers. Minimizing the use of electricity by employing the most energy-efficient light source is probably the most important thing an indoor grower can do to help save the Earth.

1) High-pressure sodium (HPS) lamps are much more efficient than fluorescents and significantly more efficient than the long-tubed lights. A 4-tube, eight-foot fluorescent with electronic ballasts uses about 360 watts and emits about 30,000 lumens. A 400-watt HPS emits about 45,000 lumens, 50 percent more than the battery of fluorescents. Although there would be a slight increase in electrical usage, given good conditions plant growth would increase linearly. A 250-watt HPS lamp emits almost 25,000 lumens—83 percent of the light of the four fluorescent tubes with only 63 percent of the electricity. Over a year-long period the 250-watt HPS lamp saves about 985 kilowatt-hours. At 12 cents a kilowatt, this comes to about $118 year.

2) Make sure all the light gets to the garden. Light that is generated but lost may as well not have been emitted in the first place. Aluminum foil, Mylar, flat white paint and metallic wrapping paper have all been used to line walls. Horizontal reflectors aim the light directly at the garden and get much more of it to the plants than vertical reflectors.

3) The fertilizers used indoors are detrimental to the environment when they are flushed or drained. The best way to deal with them is to add them to a compost pile, where the bacteria and other micro-organisms will use the fertilizer to transform the pile into fertile mulch. Fertilizer can also be used outdoors as an occasional spray on the lawn and perennials, or even in the vegetable garden.

4) Most cultivation books say that planting mediums are inexpensive and

This garden in the California foothills disturbed the ecology of the area. Holes were dug and water lines stretched to the dry, thirsty soil. Since there was an extremely low water table, water had to be run to the plants constantly. To keep rodents away, the grower set several traps. The area was partially fenced as well. The silt was turned and the whole patch was planted in bare ground. This was very easy to see from the air and will take many years to repair. Topsoil will be washed away in the first rain, further ruining the space. This plot should be mulched with forest debris immediately.

should be discarded rather than re-used. The reasons given are fear of infection and the buildup of fertilizer salts. However, the medium can be cleansed of pathogens by using either heat or a sterilizing agent, such as hydrogen per-

oxide or commercial products such as Zero-Tol®. Fertilizer salts can be leached out by rinse or by soaking the medium in warm water.

Commercial vegetable and flower growers in Holland use rockwool for up to 18 months before replacing it. After each crop, they rinse it and remove the large roots. After the rockwool is too deteriorated for use indoors, it goes on permanent duty lining the bottom and sides of planting holes dug for trees and large perennials. The rockwool captures more water than soil would, and keeps the root zone moist for longer periods between irrigations.

Potting mixes with vermiculite, perlite, compost, peat moss and other fill can be soaked by first placing the material in a fine net bag, sort of a giant teabag. Some of the material disappears with each cycle and is replaced with new material. Unless the medium seems to be harboring viruses or other pathogens, it can be used for a number of years.

Exhausted planting mixes can be used in an outdoor garden. They can be added to dense loams and clay soils to loosen them up or used as a component of mixes when planting trees or other specimens for which holes are dug. They can also be mixed into compost piles, where the organic matter in the mixes will compost with the rest of the pile. The inert matter, such as perlite, will help keep it loose. The vermiculite disintegrates, adding micro-nutrients.

The ultimate mediums to use—ecologically speaking—are the permanent

ones: sand, gravel, lava and cera[...] beads. They are virtually inert, are e[...] ily washed, rinsed and sterilized, [...] never need to be replaced.

5) CO_2 gas is created by burning na[...] ral gas, a fossil hydrocarbon. CO_2 [...] also generated in the house. Gas bu[...] ers on stoves, heaters, furnaces [...] water heaters all generate CO_2, wh[...] can be vented into the grow room. [...] only does this save money on the p[...] chase of gas, but it also helps con[...] the CO_2 produced in the home into [...] gen and water, helping minimize [...] greenhouse effect. Any setup wh[...] uses CO_2 generated by furnaces [...] water heaters should be installed v[...] the help of a professional to make s[...] that you and/or your plants are [...] harmed by excessive levels of car[...] monoxide (CO).

Outdoors

Guerrilla growers often have a con[...] between environmental correctness [...] gardening success. Land clearing, fe[...] ing, fertilizers, pesticides and hum[...] presence all have negative effects [...] the environment. What is a grower [...] do? Here are some suggestions:

1) Rather than digging in the grou[...] use planting bags filled with medi[...] This way the ground is not affected [...] much. The containers can be pla[...] anywhere and moved around, giving [...] grower additional freedom in gar[...] design. This comes in especially ha[...] should the location need to [...] changed.

2) Like other farmers, marijuana gr[...] ers are often in competition w[...] wildlife. It is one thing to place mat[...] al near the garden that repels pests. [...] is quite another to trap the creatu[...] and still worse to poison them, si[...] poison usually winds its way throu[...] the ecosystem (and frequently back [...] us). There is no reason to kill whe[...] preventive measure will suffice. Rat[...] than fencing off an area from anim[...] growers may be able to place the pla[...] at a level where they cannot be reac[...] by deer and/or other ground-based h[...] bivores. The boughs of trees make go[...] spots. Some natural outcrop formatio[...]

and abandoned architecture can also be used for this purpose.

When plants are small, barriers can be placed over them to prevent predation. A tent-like structure of thin cloth seals out insects and other chewers. Tomato cages or poultry wire can stop rodents and deer.

One grower had been unable to bring in a crop because of animals. Rats had chewed the stems of the first transplants, and deer were eating the leaves. He used a 12-volt negative ion generator with storage battery and solar recharge. He attached the output to the stem using electric cord. Animals that touched the stem or leaves received a mild tingling shock and quickly learned to stay away.

3) Getting water to the plants can also cause environmental damage. Trail and drip lines wreak havoc on sensitive ecologies. Trampled plants, compacted ground and unnaturally moist ground can cause serious damage. Instead of bringing the water in, it is much more ecologically-minded to plant in areas where no additional water is needed; along streams and canals, near natural springs, or on ground which holds enough moisture between rainfalls.

If additional water is needed, a simple cistern might be sufficient. It can be made from rigid plastic or plastic film, much like a waterbed mattress. It is not difficult to make a water-conserving wick or reservoir hydroponic container. These units hold all the water they are given. No water percolates into the ground and there is virtually no evaporation, so much less is required. The only concern is making a large enough reservoir.

If you dig, adding water-retaining crystals to the soil may actually help the environment. These commercially available crystals swell to many times their weight when exposed to water, and release moisture gradually to the surrounding drying medium.

4) If police energy is taken up with decoy plants, they have less time and resources to devote to indoor gardens and hidden patches. Seeds can be tossed anywhere. Of course, the plant has a much better chance of growing a few inches if it is placed in the ground as a transplant. This might also be a suitable use for orphan males.

This grow room used three kilowatts per hour, but the parabolic reflectors were not as efficient as horizontals would have been. Also, large plants were incorrect for this light. They took too long to grow, and the light could not reach below the top canopy, so the extra plant weight was of no benefit. Light was lost to the sides, since there was space between the plants and a two-foot aisle.

CAMOUFLAGED

America's rural areas, once retreats for those tired of the noise of civilization, now buzz each summer and fall with helicopters and low-flying planes looking for cannabis. Police use aerial and ground sightings to obtain warrants. Penalties are stiff and confiscation can eliminate a whole season's work. But it's not difficult to camouflage your plants. All it takes is some imagination and a little bit of effort.

GARDENS
hiding the crop

This wild hedge at the perimeter of the garden is an ideal spot for camouflaging marijuana plants. The morning glory flowers decrease the attention paid to the greenery.

ALTHOUGH POLICE have been very successful spotting gardens, it's not always the plants that tip them off. Trails, litter and other signs of human habitation, visible irrigation pipes and disturbed ground are all clues for law enforcement.

Buried irrigation tubing can be detected at night using infrared scanners. The water remaining in the tubing cools the above ground, which looks like veins over the land in infrared photos. If the tubing is in a hilly area it can be drained each time it is used. The air left in the tubes does not cause nearly as much temperature differentiation. In order for this to be effective, irrigation has to be done early in the day so the ground has a chance to heat up again after the tubing is drained.

Trails are easily seen from both air and road. If a trail leads to a person's residence, courts generally infer a connection. If a grower takes a different approach to the garden each time, no apparent trail develops. One way to break a trail is to design it so that it is blocked by tall, thick bushes and then have it meander off to nothingness. The trick is that the entrance is blocked by impenetrable bushes that can be lifted up, revealing the entrance to a tunnel carved through the bush using a chain saw and hedge clippers.

> "There is little that the gardener can do to change the color of cannabis, but color can be used as a means of camouflage."

Cops often notice tell-tale grow paraphernalia first, then look for the garden. Bottles, wrappers and paper all may stand out even from 500 or 1000 feet above. In one case, the only connection between the accused and the garden was cigarette butts with ends bitten in a particular way that were found at both the garden and the accused's home. The grower pled to a reduced charge rather than risk trial. Always carry all your garbage out. All wrappers, boxes, trays, bags and broken equipment should be removed from the garden each time it is visited. From the air, cleared or disturbed ground is very obvious. It stands out against foliage and is naturally a cause of suspicion. To avoid detection, growers typically strew the site with dead vegetation. This may not be enough. One way to regreen the site quickly is to plant a fast-germinating cover crop such as grass or clover. Within a few days the first green will appear, and within weeks the grass will naturalize. Another grower used a piece of green burlap to cover the ground. In addition to providing camouflage, the burlap acted much like mulch by keeping the ground cool against the sun.

Marijuana comes in many shades of green, depending on the variety and stage of growth as well as environmental conditions. In areas where there is little or no rain during the summer, the intense green of the irrigated plants often stands out against the surrounding vegetation. Even in areas where there is plenty of rain during the summer, problems may occur in the fall, when the surrounding foliage changes color more than cannabis, leaving a green plant in the midst of autumn shades.

There is little that the gardener can do to change the color of cannabis, but color can be used as a means of camouflage. Growers sometimes attach flowers to the plants. These can be artificial flowers or just colored tissues held onto the plant using twist-ties. Since cannabis does not grow large flowers, a fully "flowered" plant is well disguised.

Another grower let morning glories climb over the plants in a very controlled fashion. This changed both the

These plants were pruned to blend in with the garden's perennial bushes.

This shed is mounted on wheels and rail. At the slightest sign of police helicopter activity one person can roll the metal building right over the plants in about 90 seconds, protecting them from view. It is a convenient way to protect the plants from rain, and can also be used to force plants to flower out of season. Mounted with lights, it can be used to supplement short days during the winter.

configuration of the plants and added blue flowers. Nasturtiums can also be used, and they have very bright flowers. Changing the shape of the plant is another way to disguise cannabis. Police are looking for plants with the classic Christmas-tree form. Plants can be pruned or bent over so that the main stem lies on the ground. One grower shaped her plants by wrapping them in agricultural netting. Another grower trimmed the ends from each pointy leaf to disguise its telltale cannabis shape. He kept his plants bushy by trimming them so they would branch.

Late planting can also prevent detection (see the article "On Late Planting," page 38). Police look for plants three feet tall and larger, and generally keep their sights too high. Seedlings or clones planted in mid-August often grow to only 2 feet and have very little branching. One grower started a small patch of indicas in mid-August. The six-inch clones grew an additional foot before they ripened in early October. They were placed about nine inches apart and there was only one long bud on each plant.

Context can also be a disguise. The backyard of a home in the suburbs of Atlanta was surrounded by perennial bushes which stayed green all year. One year several new "bushes" were added. All summer long, a hedge clipper was used to keep the "bushes" rounded and to encourage branching. Neighbors who came to barbecues had no idea that they were sitting just 10 feet away from cannabis. A gardener in New Jersey alternated tomato plants with marijuana plants in his vegetable garden. Another farmer in Minnesota waited till the corn was high, then transferred his cannabis plants in between the rows. The trick, he said, was making sure the plants stayed shorter than the corn.

Smart cultivators camouflage themselves, too. Always have a good cover in case the police stop you tramping through the woods. Nature trips, herb collecting, photography and dog walking are all pretenses to maintain. A fellow I know dresses up as a hunter to go harvesting.

This plant can blend into a diverse environment fairly easily. Cops are looking for plants with a "distinctive green" color. This suspect doesn't fit the profile. It looks like it could be a decorative garden plant.

These plants were placed in growing holes and blend in with the environment. From the air they looked like young trees.

Marijuana planted in an area with perennial bushes. It will not stand out in the fall because the surrounding leaves will turn fall colors.

HOMER'S GUERILLA

I was a guerrilla grower. Actually I was a breeder more than a grower, I grew seed crops each year, trying to improve the quality of the smoke. I've never done any large-scale patches. I grew lots of small patches over a 100-square-mile radius. It was a full-time job winter and summer. During the spring, summer and fall I traveled all over the area by car and motorcycle. In the winter, I manicured pot and fixed the vehicles for the upcoming season. I didn't take a vacation for 5 years. Doing this was my vacation.

GARDEN
heavenly high yields

THE MAIN INGREDIENT to successful guerilla growing is finding a number of locations that are truly secret and that also have water, sun and soil. I was continually looking for new locations. The situation was constantly changing. For instance, you may pull a crop off one year and then the next, loggers come into an area in the woods and discover the patch. Surveyors, forest firefighters, hunters and other guerilla farmers working close to an area make it unsuitable for use. I rented a helicopter during the winter for a few hours just to see what you could see from 1000 and 1500 feet. You can see everything. I passed one patch from the sky where the guy had left fertilizer sacks flapping in the bushes. CAMP (Campaign Against Marijuana Planting) busted that patch.

The helicopter ride changed my modus operandi. Keep it small and unobtrusive. It must be totally undetectable from the air and that's an impossibility unless the patch is underneath trees and then the plants don't have sun. You have to take what the environment gives you without taking more than it has to offer. When you change the environment, cut things down, move stuff around too much or dig the place up a lot, it is very obvious from the air. You can plant someplace you think

they won't look. That's a gamble though, because you can only guess where they don't look. My plan was to plant where I thought they wouldn't look, but also to make it hard for them to see if they did. I kept the plots small and left the environment as undisturbed as possible.

The main ingredient to successful guerilla growing is finding a number of locations that are truly secret and that also have water, sun and soil.

There is virtually no summer rain where I grew, so the plants had to be irrigated. Other guerilla farmers use pumps and machinery to move water to their plants. I don't like to do that. Instead, I choose places near water and downhill from it. This eliminates lots of places, but with a simple gravity hose set-up there is much less chance of malfunction than with machinery. With this system, even if I didn't return for a month, the unit would still be working. You have to bury the hose to prevent rodents, bears and other wildlife from chewing on it to get the water. Bears also use the hose as dental floss. They've ruined many rolls of my stashed, but unburied hose.

Most of the other farmers who I've known grow on private property. I've always grown out in the woods on government land because of the government's property forfeiture laws. I would set up one patch and then go onto the next. I put the patches on a one-week rotation and tried to visit them once a week.

For a few years I started seeds in my backyard garden in April and continued germinating seed until the end of May. I started about 1000 plants with the idea of growing about 100 to maturity spread over 5 patches. I chose only the healthy, vigorous seedlings for transplanting, resulting in 25 to 50 viable seedlings a week. The first seedlings were ready for transplanting in late May. Each week I planted new patches

and replaced dead or missing plants in the areas I had already started.

I found I had a lot of trouble doing it this way for three reasons. The first is that the plants were exposed to cops and robbers for five months. Second, hungry animals and insects like the young tender sprouts. Third, the plants got too large when they were started this early.

After a few years I developed a new method. Around June 21, I soaked seeds for a day so they would germinate by July 1. They were placed under high-pressure sodium lamps for 3 weeks of continuous lighting. They were ripe for outdoor planting by the end of July. This kept animal damage to a minimum because they were protected indoors while they were young and tender. The plants were only outdoors for a few weeks before the shorter days of approaching autumn forced them to flower. The plants grew only 4-8 feet in height, making them less conspicuous, and they were outdoors for only ten weeks total, so there was less chance of their discovery.

I kept the plants in the garden until they were about a foot tall. At night, I would take a load out and stash it in the woods fairly close to the patch. The next day I would come back and backpack the plants in. They were in paper quart containers which I removed before planting. I would put the plants right into the ground, watering thoroughly with a water-nutrient solution. Once all the plants were in the ground I set up the irrigation system. The drip system is controlled by a battery-operated, programmable water timer. I set it to operate from two to five hours daily depending on plant size and water conditions.

demanding requirements so I don't find a lot of spots. I looked at the sites in the summer and fall rather than the winter so I could see the light and water conditions during the blooming season. The position of the sun is most important during the blooming season, in September and October. You may see beautiful sunshine in July, however, by September it will be behind the trees. Shadows during prime sun time result in air-bud. Irrigation is a must. Before CAMP, I was lucky enough to discover an area fed by springs, but these are the first places the cops check now.

> **To keep the areas undetectable, it is most important to leave no trails, debris, garbage or other signs of human disturbance.**

It was completely obvious. The new patches took more care than the ones I used previously. It was a completely new situation. I wasn't familiar with the traffic patterns of the area so I couldn't be seen running around. People would

To keep the areas undetectable, it is most important to leave no trails, debris, garbage or other signs of human disturbance. When I searched for suitable grow spots, I found pot patches all the time because the growers left signs of their presence. Trails serve as highways leading to most patches. Stuff laying around, cut trees and other vegetation acts as dead wood lying around like markers. I've found trails by the beer cans and candy wrappers tossed by the gardeners. The people didn't even realize that they were signing their trail.

The last transplants were in the ground by the first week of August. Then I had to maintain the patches—to see that the plants got adequate amounts of water and nutrients for the next few months. The ground was pretty dry. A lot of areas were browning out. They wouldn't be green again until the fall rains. I was constantly on the road checking the patches and getting the bugs out of the irrigation system. A filter on a system plugged up totally after three days. In sandy soil, a large filter that won't plug up is better. If the filter is too small and plugs, the ground (and plants) will go dry. I fertilized and got my routine together.

I spent my spare time looking for new places to grow next year. I have

say, "What's this clown up to?" People in the countryside take notice of people and cars randomly coming and going. I like to find four or five different ways of getting to the area so that I'm not noticed.

After I found a spot, I had to set it up. Tools had to be carried in (I generally leave them in the area so that I don't have to carry them around). The irrigation system had to be set up. I like to do this as late as possible so that no stuff is lying around for people to stumble upon. Then I had to figure out the watering pattern. I saw how wet the soil stayed, and adjusted the drip to meet the plant's needs.

Ram pumps use the stream's energy to pump a small amount of water uphill. They take a lot of maintenance because sturdy, reliable equipment is heavy and impossible to pack in. This leaves only the flimsiest plastic models, which constantly break down. They also make a lot of noise, In 1984 I used a ram pump, but it was discovered by

hikers and I haven't used one since. This got me on my trip of looking for water uphill from a plot. It makes things so much easier.

Summer is a busy time for me. I drive as much as 75 miles between patches. Then I use one of my three stashed motorcycles to get closer to the garden. Hopefully it's all routine work: checking out the irrigation lines, looking for signs of human presence. I am careful not to leave any signs of myself.

By the middle of the month I knew that it was going to be a really dry year. In one patch, which I ran the previous year, I found a pond that was able to supply all the plants. But by the middle of July it was obvious that the pond would not have enough water to irrigate all of the plants at one time. I split the irrigation line in two. Each part watered half the garden. This way there was no danger that the hose would lose its siphon, but I had to visit the garden twice as often to switch the irrigation lines. This increased my risk of being spotted or noticed by locals.

For me the most exciting part is watching the plants grow. Each day the plants grew several inches and bushed out. Starting as one-foot-tall transplants, the girls had grown to four, six-foot adolescents. In early July, I started pruning the larger plants that had been placed outdoors in late May. I pruned the plants vigorously, cutting the six footers back to four feet, but this was only a temporary constraint to them. If plants are pruned after July 15, they do not have enough time to form areas so the yield is reduced dramatically.

The stigmas, the erect white hairs, began to appear translucent and moist, glistening in the sunlight. I watched the sun

setting on the horizon. It was a fiery ball sending its red rays east across the valley stretching for 50 miles. The stigmas caught the rays and lit up with a fierce glow, shouting, "We Are Here! We Are Here!" I don't know what I feel. Is it their determination to be alive? A plant, which would wither without the water I give it, affirming life. Or is it the drive to reproduce? These are but the first of many flowers to scour the air for the male's pollen.

This is the last time I will see my plants for several weeks. One full day's work in the garden, I check the siphon lines leading to the plot, adjust the flow so there is a constant trickle and then add a natural fertilizer mix I purchased,

which is made of rock powders and seed meals. I add some aged guano containing lots of phosphorus to promote flowering. I dig it into the soil to a depth of about four inches in a ring around the plant. The plants will get a little nutrient tea with the water trickle. I stake the plants at the base.

The sun goes down and I hike out of the woods. I am wearing heavyweight jeans and a canvas jacket. I have on a pair of comfortable work gloves, I am wearing a bandana around my neck and a lightweight cap with flaps over my ears. Only my face is showing and that is lathered with mosquito repellent. I am using a good walking stick from an outdoors shop. My small knapsack contains a bag with soil samples neatly marked with the location from which they were taken and depth. I have my western field guide to endogenous plants and I have a little viewer as well as a point and shoot camera with a roll of exposed film with recent shots of the area taken for research purposes.

With all this gear, I don't use a trail. I know my bike is due east and I start walking through the woods to the road. At the 53 marker I walk 10 yards in, and wheel out my Suzuki. I'm out of there.

Around August 1, the males start to show, and I remove them as soon as I detect them. The plants were growing very close together and I cut them down rather than pulling them up so that I would not disturb the females' roots. Detecting the males early, before the flowers open, greatly reduces the chance of letting any pollen get air-

borne. Once the flowers open, it is better to place a plastic bag over the plant and then cut it. It's already bagged for removal.

I had to check on males several times a week. Since I am more of a breeder than a grower, I kept two males in another patch, which also contained seven females. This was certainly a dichotomy. I was cutting down males in the patches only to return in a couple of weeks to the same patches bearing pollen to fertilize selected females.

I find that if you have a potent plant to begin with, the difference between the stone of sinsemilla compared to moderately seeded pot is insignificant. The biggest difference is in the taste. Lightly seeding pot insures the continuation of the seedline. It assures everyone, customer and grower alike, that there will be seeds for next year's crop. But the customer is more interested in cosmetic appearance. Lightly seeded pot is harder to clean because it contains immature seed bits and is harder to roll—the seeds must be removed. It's a lot harder to remove seeds from resinous bud than from Columbian.

I was back in the garden four weeks later. I came at twilight and spent the night there in my sleeping bag. Then in the morning I woke up with the sun creating a tiny dome in the eastern horizon. It was orange, not the deepening red-orange of the setting sun, but the orange, almost yellow, presaging a white burn.

The orange-tinted early light turned the greens of the clearing shades to brown, then tan. Fifteen minutes later, the sun

lost its color and turned molten white. The garden's colors appeared. Native, dull greens. Greens looking hardened against the summer sun's daily onslaught and the annual summer drought. Tough greens, olive greens, gray greens. The flattened faded greens of live oaks, madrones, firs, mullein and other dry weather plants, survival plants with deep roots seeking the last bits of moisture from the parched ground.

The boundary between the cracked earth, baked into hard blocks, and the friable earth of the garden is just an inch. Inside the oasis, my plants are shimmering bright green. They are in their own little world, oblivious to the dryness around them. The eight plants' roots thrive in the moist succored garden, unaware of their dependence on the half-inch water hose constantly trickling life-giving water.

The few stigmas that I saw a month ago have multiplied many times. First they grew into groups, then clumps. Then new flushes of flowers squeezed the older stigmas as they stretched out in a desperate attempt to seek pollen. Even more stigmas popped. The clumps, once distinct and separate growths, have merged into giant colas stretching over a foot, hiding the stem. The branches no longer look green. The white bud puffs hide the green leaves.

It was 9 am. The day was beginning to heat up. It had already climbed from the low 60's at 6 am to 80 degrees. I spent the last three hours cleaning out the drippers and staking the plants. The sky was a clear deep blue with no

clouds at all. I sat down in the dubious shade of a 6-foot plant to drink some water, and looked around and listened. The site is a mile into forest and the sounds of humans are very distant: an occasional auto, some machinery. The stillness of the breezeless summer scene is overpowering. Everything is dominated by the sun. It was already too bright to view without sunglasses. I was wearing my hat with the neck flaps and long sleeve protection, with plenty of cotton to absorb the sweat. I filled the pint container from the hose a second time and drank it down. Then I filled another one, drank half, and poured the rest over my face.

It took about a minute to fill a container. I waited patiently then put the refilled container in my mini-pack, planted the sleeping bag in the hidden crotch of an old tree and hiked to my bike.

The second stage of flowering began when the hairs started to turn color. First they lost a little translucence, and had the opaque look of fine bone china. Then the stigmas stained with the slightest tints of yellow, red or purple but they remained moist looking. Over a period of two weeks they developed deeper color and became opaque. Then the stigmas began to dry. The glands swelled a bit and the resins became apparent. There was a hint of sparkle as the glands started forming on the bud's surfaces.

At the bottom of the cola, the hairs formed wrinkled shapes of opaque red threads as they dried. They contrasted starkly against the dull green vegetation. The buds in the middle of the cola stuck out brightly in the sun, glowing deep shades of red. The hairs at the top were still mostly white; only

a few of them had turned red. They were almost ready to harvest. The leaves started to lose their green color, turning bright yellow.

Some paranoid farmers harvest at the second stage of flowering. They figure the flowers are mature, they will put on only a little more weight, so why take a chance by keeping the plants out in the field? The reason is that there is a difference between immature and ripe plants. The plants do not reach their peak potency and taste until they fluoresce with glands full of mature resins.

There is a good reason why people harvest early: fear of losing the crop to the drug task forces hunting gardens. In California, most rural counties have an anti-drug task force outfitted with planes, helicopters and grown men playing teenage ninjas. They fly around all summer noting patches. Occasionally they make an easy bust with the help of the sheriff's department, but mostly they mark the locations on a map for CAMP (Campaign Against Marijuana Planting) actions. CAMP crews, composed of cowboys, roam the state. They come into each county for a short period late in the summer after all the information has been gathered, but before plants are ready for harvest.

Since 1984, they have been using Huey-type helicopters to bring in crews and haul out pot. The helicopters have a hoist which can move large loads. Then the crew walks to the next patch if it is close or reboards to move to the next field. When the helicopter is filled up, it empties its load into a dump truck located on an accessible road.

The search planes do the once-over for the entire territory, but concentrate on areas where lots of hippies are known

to live. In one part of the county, the planes and helicopters fly back and forth in a north–south grid. When they are done, they go east–west.

The worst raid that ever occurred was in Denny, California in 1981. Almost everybody was growing in their backyard. It was right out in the open and upfront. CAMP used a paramilitary operation. First, they barricaded the roads to the town and severed telephone lines. Then, they made forced-entry searches of homes and yards. They threatened the residents with pointed weapons, harassed kids and created mayhem. As a result of lawsuits following the raid, police actions in the area were overseen by a federal court for many years.

The Denny operation started in the center of town and spiraled out into the mountains. My patch was about three miles away from the raid. I went to the patch, fertilized and checked the irrigation lines. I heard the helicopters and vehicles all afternoon but I never saw them. Two days later, I went to a patch 15 miles away and it had been harvested. That was the first patch I ever lost to CAMP. They spent only one day in my area but they got about 60 percent of the crop. Most of the growers were inexperienced city people and they didn't know how to conceal the plants or themselves. They left highways to their patches, and didn't realize how much can be seen from the air.

Yes. September was the hardest month. The plants were ripening and were worth being ripped off. If anyone knew where they were, I could expect them to steal them. It was pretty much a waiting game. I'd go to the patch—if it was still there, I'd take care of what I had to do. If it wasn't there, it wasn't there, and there was nothing I could do about it.

Although the plants weren't quite ready, they were already valuable. Rip-offs don't wait to take them. If they didn't get them already, they didn't know where they were and they wouldn't get them. The main thing left to worry about was the stray hunter or hiker who might have stumbled upon them. I was getting pretty good at picking my places.

At this stage I had to travel more alertly between my patches. The males of the late sativas were beginning to ripen and I didn't want them to pollinate my earlier ripening indicas. I planted different varieties in each patch so that I could harvest some each time I visited. This was easier than having to harvest the whole patch at once.

It was early September but the sheriff had a new spurt of energy. Spurred by hunters' reports, he and his deputies made periodic forays into the countryside. Most of the patches they seized were small ones near the roads. But there are still walkers left among the hunters.

In mid-September the storm hit. Usually I have the plants tied up and staked by the time the winds and rains start. But this storm was two weeks early and strong. All of the patches sustained damage and many of the plants were knocked down. A few plants were beyond saving. They didn't have much bud but I was able to salvage a little bit. I threw the plants away, out of the patch. I tied up the

rest of the plants as best I could. I hauled brush in so that the plants I couldn't tie up rested on the piles underneath for support. I staked a few, and gave the broken branches splints.

Once plants are knocked down, the branches are pushed closer together. They have to be separated or they will not get the air circulation required to keep them free from mold. The molds attack as soon as dew and storms present a moist environment.

September is the driest month as far as irrigation goes. The streams nearly run dry as the yearly drought continues. I always had enough. The streams I used never actually ran out. The recent storm helped the level for only a week or so. But it also created a lot of silt, which plugs up the irrigation system. The filters had to be cleaned weekly.

Once you get through CAMP, you've got a pretty good chance of making it. However, as soon as CAMP splits, the deer-hunting season starts. Hunters are walking all over the woods. I've had people walk within a hundred feet of a patch. I've seen their tracks. People sometimes don't recognize it though, and I was lucky. The hunters are well aware of what's going on and generally steal what they find. Sometimes they turn it in. California hunting licenses warn people to be on the lookout for patches.

During the final stage, the ovary behind each hair swells into a false seed pod as the dried thread shrinks. The crystals—actually the swelling glands—shine all over the bud, creating a breathtaking fluorescence. The

glands capture each ray of light, concentrate it and send out rays of diamond light. In the mornings it had an orange tinge, much like topaz; during the day, like blue diamonds and at night I saw ruby tones. It was a dazzling display. The resins were just beginning to lose their clarity, turning amber. The leaves were turning brown as they dried up. It was time to start harvesting.

The first to mature were the Durban crosses, which were ripe in late September. Most of these were Durban-Afghans. They were filling out well and the leaves were beginning to fall off. More importantly, they were really sticky.

I like to let the plants flower for eight weeks. That way, I'm sure that the bud is ripe. I know that some varieties mature in less time, but they don't over-ripen from hanging out. They just get riper, and, I believe, stonier. It's only in those last few weeks that the resins mature.

I took the first three out of one patch. First I cut them up at the patch so that they would fit into a large plastic leaf-and-garden/garbage bag. I threw away the long bare branches. Then I put all of the colas into the bag and carried them out of the patch. I took them back to the drying area and hung them up.

During the first week of October, I spent my time checking the ripening plants. The main harvest began around October 7th, then reaping continued. I visited each garden about once a week. I cut the plants that were ready to harvest, leaving the big stalks at the

site and packing out only the bud. I could carry rough trimmed bud from six to eight plants pretty easily. But it's a hard hike in and out—rough country and a lot a climbing, so larger harvests required more than one trip.

I was harvesting from three large bud patches and a small seed patch. Once I hiked out, I cycled with the pack to the drying area.

The first step was to trim the branches. The fan leaves contain a tremendous amount of water and increase the humidity of the dry area tremendously. At the same time, they block the air from circulating around the bud. I removed the fan leaves using curved blade stainless steel manicuring scissors. Friends of mine would just pinch them off with their nails. Moisture escapes at an accelerated rate from the wound area. Once the big leaves are off, I hung the colas using the joint between a bud and the stem as the crotch.

In the middle of the month I checked the sites and brought back another load. Going to one plot I saw hunter's tracks on the other side of the field. Had they been pot conscious, they certainly would have recognized it, but fortunately, they kept on their tracks.

Detecting the males early, before the flowers open, greatly reduces the chance of letting any pollen get airborne.

This placed me in a dilemma; it didn't look like anybody had been there because there were no tracks in the patch, but they might have seen it and be planning to take some sort of action later. Harvest it all now or leave what's not ripe? I took the second course and stuck with my karma and intuition.

By the end of October, the main part of the harvest was complete and all that was left to harvest was the seed patch and the late sativas, which I grew for personal stash. I prefer them to the indicas.

The final yield was substantial, with only small losses to the government

and none to rip-offs. The plants yielded between 1/2 and 1 pound each and were very potent.

The problem with breeding while guerilla growing is that you have no control over the environment. I eliminated all but the best male in the seed patch, and trimmed it so that it produced only a moderate amount of pollen and the buds were only partially seeded. After a couple of weeks of flowering it was removed. That way, only the first flowers—usually at the base where the branch met the stem—were pollinated, leaving the rest of the bud sinsemilla. I collected about 30 seeds per plant.

My method was simple. The male would pollinate all the females within 60 feet. I chose the best male after considering factors such as early maturity, shape, robustness, odor and glands that showed. All the plants in the patch were pollinated. After smoking each of the females, I decided which plants' seeds to keep. This was based mainly on the plant's stoniness rather than yield. Only the exceptional were propagated the next year. I had started with indica and African seed as well as other varieties. However my hybridization created a totally unique plant which was well adapted to the mountains of northern California.

OUTDOOR

Hydroponic systems for the outdoor grower have several advantages over conventional gardening methods. They are easy to set up and can be placed virtually anywhere it is convenient to grow. The soil conditions are not important and there is no digging or spadework involved. Once set up, a hydroponic system requires much less water than a soil-bound plant garden.

HYDROPONICS
soilless gardening

MAINTENANCE IS EASY because there is usually no need for a drip line. No water is lost to the ground and little evaporates. Hydroponic units water the plants automatically and use water and nutrients extremely efficiently. These conditions encourage fast growth because the plants receive more than adequate amounts of nutrients, water and oxygen. This is very helpful outdoors where the plants receive very intense light and where a lack of water and nutrients often limits growth.

Rockwool can be used to set up an easy hydro system. The plants were started in 4 inch rockwool cubes. These were placed on larger rockwool pads once the roots grew through the block. They were watered using drip emitters that delivered nutrient-enriched water to the plants.

Finally, hydroponic systems are portable and can be moved or removed quickly without disturbing the plants' roots. Remember that there are lots of reasons for wishing to move a plant besides safety. The sun's position changes seasonally so a portable plant can always be placed in the best light.

In remote areas, hydroponic units have advantages over conventional garden methods. They use one-third or less water than plants growing in the ground or in conventional containers because none is lost in the soil. Instead it is held in a container until used by the plant. Only a small percentage evaporates from the top. Systems can be designed to capture and hold huge amounts of water, so visits can be infrequent. Gardens in areas with summer rainfall can refill their tanks automatically by using a small catchment system and a tank or cistern.

There are several hydroponic systems that are easy to construct, so you can make your own. There are quite a few books on the subject. The simplest systems to construct and maintain are the "reservoir system" and the "wick system." These passive systems regulate water supply with no electricity and few moving parts. When the containers are on one level, a single float valve can be hooked up to a large reservoir. Individual float valves are used if the containers are on different levels. Both the wick system and the reservoir system promote rapid plant growth.

The wick system uses a 3/8-inch woven nylon rope as a wick. The rope is cut long enough so that it hangs from both drain holes into a reservoir below, which is filled with water–nutrient solution. The container is filled with a moist planting medium such as vermiculite–perlite, or peat or bark-based planting mixes. Water is drawn up from a bottom reservoir by capillary

action so the planting mix stays moist continually.

The reservoir system is even simpler. It consists of a container sitting in a shallow pool of water–nutrient solution. For example, a twelve-inch-tall container will sit in three inches of liquid. The containers are filled with a dry medium such as clay planting pellets, lava rock or a vermiculite–perlite–sand mix. Sometimes a float valve is used to regulate water coming from a gravity-fed reservoir. The units can be dug into the ground or left above as the situation requires.

Some people find it more convenient to buy one of the many hydroponic units available commercially. Most of them use a drip system, an ebb-and-flow method, or a nutrient-flow technique (NFT) of water delivery. These systems generally work well and take little time to set up, but they can be used only where there is a source of electricity to run the pumps. Since the pump takes little energy to recirculate the water, it can be powered from a marine battery or solar pump. Recirculating drip systems pump water from the reservoir through the drip emitters to the tops of containers. Ebb-and-flow systems flood the tray(s) with water and then let it drain back to the reservoir. NFT systems send a constant flow of water over the roots so they are constantly irrigated with oxygen-rich water.

During the day, sunlight can heat the water to the point where it cooks the roots. Dark and black-colored reservoirs are the worst because they absorb all the light and turn it into heat. Colored trays also heat the water. The darker the tray's color, the more heat it absorbs. White reflects the light and stays cool. In the fall, the water may cool off a little too much at night since the roots do best above 65 degrees. An aquarium heater will keep the water warm during cool periods.

There are several other ways to modify the reservoir's water temperature. The first is to mulch the reservoir so the sun's strong rays never reach its surface. Earth, stones, sand, vegetative debris or living plants can be used. Another method is to time the irrigations so that the plants are watered only during the times of day when the water is within the proper range. One farmer hooked his pump directly to a solar battery. The plants were irrigated gently as the sun rose. As the sun's rays got stronger towards midday, the pump worked harder. As the rays waned later in the day, the pump stopped. It remained inactive in the evening.

There are many brands of hydroponic fertilizers. Each brand has its fans and followers. The advantage of the hydros over conventional fertilizers is that they provide all the nutrients that plants require and are formulated specifically for water delivery systems. Water conditions vary greatly around the country. For that reason, a fertilizer formula that performs well in one area may do poorly in an area with different water conditions. Conventional fertilizers are formulated to react with soil or planting mix and do very poorly in hydro solutions.

The light is much more intense outdoors during the summer than in indoor gardens, so plant growth is much denser and faster. In sunlit gardens, the plant's water and nutrient requirements are also much greater. The units must be irrigated more frequently so that the plants do not become water-stressed. During the long warm days of summer, when plants use more water, it is best to err in favor of irrigating more often than not. If the nutrient solution is the same strength during the warm months as during cooler periods, the plants will receive too much fertilizer. During the hot periods dilute the fertilizer a bit. Even though nutrient needs rise, water use increases and the plants will absorb more dilute fertilizer. This prevents over-fertilization. Since both heat and high phosphorus

(P) encourage vertical growth, the fertilizer should have a lower percentage of phosphorus than nitrogen (N).

During the autumn, as the temperature drops below 70 F and the sun's intensity wanes, plants' water requirements decline. The fertilizer solution should be made a bit stronger so that the plants are able to get adequate nutrients while using less water. At this phase, the fertilizer should have more P than N to encourage flowering. Most flowering formulas meet this requirement.

Yields from hydroponic systems are usually bigger than from plants in the ground because they don't experience the micro-stresses of conventional gardening. All of the plants' water and nutrient needs are met hydroponically. A hydroponic system in combination with intense sunlight will optimize any plant's potential.

GALLERY

GALLERY

ON LATE

By late July, most outdoor growers have completed planting. In the warmest parts of the U.S. plants may have already been in the ground for as long as three months. Plants in northerly areas have likely been in terra firma for about a month. During this time, plants have required attention, including watering, fertilizing, trimming and camouflaging as they grow into large beauties. They are also vulnerable to hungry animals, rip-offs and police.

PLANTING
covert gardening

ALL OF THESE PROBLEMS serve as deterrents to many people who would like to grow in their backyard or garden but think the plants will grow into giants that are quite obvious. There is a path out of this garden dilemma.

The solution, growers have discovered, is to start late in the season. The plants grow for only a short time before the long nights and short days force them into flowering. When plants are placed outdoors in late July or early August, they only have a month or so of vegetative growth before they begin the flowering regimen. They ripen at about the same time as larger plants of the same variety that were in the ground earlier. They are outside for less time, are much smaller than most plants and do not fit the plant profile sought out by police or thieves.

Gardens that are planted late are also easier to camouflage. They can be outfitted with paper flowers, bent or kept as single stems. Because they are not monstrous in size, they are workable and controllable without too much effort. One grower read reports that agents are instructed to look for a cer-

> **"Plants that have been grown in-doors should be exposed to sunlight gradually."**

tain color in identifying marijuana. He actually painted his plants with a thin flour water mixture. They looked a little gray or whitish from the air. He could have also added a bit of food coloring to the mix and given the leaves a tint. He said he couldn't have done that with large plants.

Getting a Late Start

To start a late garden, seedlings or clones are grown so that they are about a foot tall and ready to be placed in their outdoor location around the first week of August. Indicas, early sativas and most domestics hybrids will begin flowering almost immediately upon being placed outdoors, and will reach a height of 2 to 4 feet at maturation. They will not be very bushy. If they are placed outdoors in mid-August they will

Marijuana was transplanted into the garden around
August 1, but was almost ripe by the end of September.

go into flowering faster and will not grow nearly as tall.

Plants that ripen later, such as equatorials and late Skunks, are transplanted even later in the season—late August through late September, about the same time they are usually triggered to flower by the daily dark periods of nearly 12 hours. Of course, these varieties can only be used in the southern tier, where there is no frost through the beginning

of December or later.

Areas with no frost and warm winters, such as parts of Florida and southern California, can support plant growth throughout the year. During winter there is less than 12 hours of sun from September 22 until March 22. Both short- and long-season plants are forced to flower as soon as they are placed outside during this time of year. In Hawaii, these are called 60-day wonders, but they can be grown in some other places.

"The plants grow for only a short time before the long nights and short days force them into flowering."

Once indica plants reach a flowering threshold, they may stop most branch growth and quit getting taller, placing their energy into reproductive growth in the form of flowers. They remain very small. When they are placed in the ground, indica plants should be at least half the size that is desired at harvest.

Sativa plants, which grow in equatorial regions, respond very slowly to light cues. This is because there is little change in the number of hours of light throughout the year at 0 latitude. Speaking from experience, these plants typically don't respond to light cues until the light cycle reaches 14 hours of darkness. This makes them impractical for all but the most southern part of the U.S. where they will ripen during December or January.

Sativas are useful as winter crops in subtropical areas. If they are planted in early August they will continue to grow and may reach a fairly large size before they begin to flower. But when they are planted after September they will begin to flower while continuing to grow. They will ripen by late January or early February and will be somewhat shorter than if they were planted earlier. Indica/sativa hybrids continue to grow vegetatively to varying degrees during the early stages of flowering. Even a relatively small clone planted in early August can grow into a small bush by the time it is ripe. When sativas are planted after September, they will immediately start to flower, but will also continue to grow a little, increasing their size by 50 to 100 percent.

Both indicas and indica/sativa hybrids are good candidates for late summer planting. The indica grows compactly until it makes a transition to flowering growth. The indica/sativa hybrid continues to grow while it flowers. As both types remain relatively small, they are not so easily spotted from the air. Even if they are, they may not be recognized because the spotters are usually looking for larger plants.

Moving Indoor Plants Out

Plants relocated in the middle of the summer face peak stresses. It's hot; the sun's light is intense and includes high levels of ultraviolet (UV) light. This is the part of the sun's rays that cause tanning and sunburn. If the plants have been grown outdoors for transplanting they will not have a hard time adjusting to their new location.

The plants in the back field were planted outdoors in early June. They were forced to flower almost immediately. The black plastic was placed over the steel framing each evening and removed each morning so the plants received only 12 hours of light daily. They will be harvested in about a week on August 10. Then new plants will be planted in their place. The plants in the foreground were transplanted as cuttings July 15. They are being forced to flower early, too.

Left: These plants grew into small bushes, not marijuana's stereotypical shape, so they are harder to detect. Right: These plants were trimmed and pruned to make them look less suspicious.

Indoor plants are protected from this intense UV light. When exposed to the summer sun, they burn. This can kill the plants. Plants that have been grown indoors should be exposed to sunlight gradually. They can be hardened over a period of a week to 10 days by gradually introducing them to sunlight. The regimen should start with shaded light followed by weak morning or late afternoon light and work up to intense midday light. A shade cloth can also be used to help them adjust. Cloudy, rainy periods are an especially good time to transplant both indoor and outdoor plants.

Shade cloth is available in various percentages of shading. A 30 to 50 percent shade cloth would help make the transition much less stressful for tender plants. It can be removed once the plants have adjusted. Spray-on anti-transpirants are available at garden shops. They cover the stomata so the plant releases less water and becomes less stressed. These products are made especially for this use and are very effective.

The soil into which the plants are transplanted should be moist so the roots do not dry out when they touch it. Garden shops sell water-holding crystals that are added to the soil mix. These expand up to 200 times their dry size when they are moistened. As the soil dries, they release the water.

Gardeners using these crystals may need to water only half as often.

Plants that are bushing out too much can be pruned so that the plants do not have the usual shape. One way of changing plant shape is to knock down the main stem when it has reached a length of 3 to 4 feet. The new growth immediately changes its pattern as a result of hormones in the plant. The branches start growing vertically. Instead of a single, long main stalk, several short branches appear, looking more like a native bush than a hemp plant.

Indoor varieties of marijuana can be planted in light shade outdoors. Their growth will vary depending on the variety and degree of the shade. Northern Lights and Early Pearl fall into this category. Skunk #1, which is a very popular indoor-outdoor variety, ripens mid-season—around September 25 in the southern U.S. and October 15-30 in the

northern states and southern Canada. Crossed with the Durban series or Early Pearl it will ripen earlier. Hybridized with these two, it can tolerate light shade. When it is crossed with Haze or a late indica, its flowering will be delayed by several weeks.

Many new varieties don't grow into the traditional marijuana plant shapes. They grow bushy, into a low-growing shrub, or have other unique forms. These are easy to set in a garden situation. When they are planted out late these smaller versions are even easier to manipulate as a form of camouflage.

Although large outdoor gardens with big plants have become things of the past for the most part, plants are still being grown outdoors—either individually or in small groups. They are not as impressive to look at in the field, but the buds are the same high quality as the ones from the larger plants.

These plants were started from seed at the beginning of July. They were forced to flower after about a month of growth. Each evening they were brought into the basement and each morning they were taken outside to feast on the sun. They are pictured here at the third week of September with only two weeks to go until ripening.

REGENERATION:

When restarting a garden, marijuana gardeners usually think of using seeds or clones. Obviously, without seed there is little evolution or selection, but to the ordinary gardener, starting from seed each time is a real hassle. About half the plants are males that are useless for bud production and the females' qualities are uncertain. Although seeds give growers more control over evolution and selection, often gardeners cannot devote time and space to plants that may have quite different habits in growth, flowering time, quality and yield. One advantage of seed is that bacteria and viruses infecting a plant are not usually transferred to the seed, but they will be transferred to the clone.

THE THIRD WAY
renewing your plants

CLONES OFFER THE ADVANTAGE of uniformity. If all are taken from the same plant, they have uniform genetics. They respond to the environment uniformly: growing in the same form to approximately the same height, ripening at the same time and resulting in buds that have the same taste and potency. The problem with clones is that they can be decidedly tedious to prepare and are subject to heavy failure rates. Additionally, taking clones from clones from clones offers viruses a good opportunity to invade the plants. Some gardeners claim that "genetic drift" can be detected. This is the result of mutations, which constantly occur in living organisms. Over a period of time, slight differences can be detected in two lines of clones that have been started from the same plant.

Regrowth on previously trimmed branches. Rather than growing a few main branches, the plant bushes out. The dead leaves are old growth. They die as the new growth takes over.

In order for the plant to regenerate, some leaves must be left on the branches. Once the plants develop new branches and leaves, the old floral tissue dies.

Regenerated plants have complete infrastructures, so they can be fairly sizeable without taking up a lot of time in vegetative growth. Fewer plants, regardless of size, usually result in lighter penalties if a garden is busted.

When any plant is pruned, new leaves and branches usually begin to grow within a few weeks. Marijuana gardeners can do the same thing with their plants. The regeneration process begins at harvest. There is no seed preparation or cutting required and no planting or repotting involved. When harvesting, leave a few branches. Cut the buds but leave some leaf material and immature buds on these branches. The rest of the plant can be harvested as usual. It is important that vegetative material is left on the branches because the plant won't regenerate without them. Gardeners who wish to grow single-stem plants should remove all but one branch or leaf site on the stem and remove the other leaf sites. All of the plants' energy will focus on this remaining growth site.

Once the plants are pruned, the lights should be left on continuously. The plants will switch to the vegetative cycle and start to grow again in about 10 days. Then they can be kept in the vegetative regimen of continuous light to serve as clone mothers or they can be forced to flower when they reach the desired size.

Regenerated plants tend to sprout many branches, which results in a bushy plant with many small buds. To grow larger buds, prune the plants so that there are fewer branches. The plant will put its energy into the remaining branches, resulting in fewer but bigger buds.

There is a third way to restart your garden: regeneration. Regeneration is often faster, easier, more convenient and less labor intensive than cloning or starting with seeds. Plants that have already been harvested and are known to be high-yield females can be forced back into the vegetative cycle and then into flowering again. Yields tend to be greater, since regenerated plants have much of their infrastructure intact, including the root system and part of the stem. Another upside is that the genetics of a just harvested plant can be preserved after the harvest.

"Regeneration is often faster, easier, more convenient and less labor intensive than cloning or starting with seeds."

Most people practice regeneration only once or twice and then start again with new plants. One popular method is to harvest an indoor plant and then place it outdoors in the spring or summer. The plant regenerates and produces a fall harvest. In warmer climates you can place plants outdoors for a winter or spring harvest and then let them regenerate. If plants are forced to flower in spring or early summer using shading, they can be pruned for regeneration and they will flower again in the fall.

> **"One upside to using regeneration is that the genetics of a just-harvested plant can be preserved after the harvest."**

One woman who wrote me claimed to have a four-year-old plant that had flowered and regenerated a number of times both outdoors and indoors. She said that one spring she cut it back to make clones and left it on the porch. When she returned from a month-long trip, the plant had grown into a 3-foot-wide bush.

The space was created by blocking off part of a room using plywood and wallboard. It is lined with Mylar and plastic. It is illuminated by two 1000-watt HPS lamps, which create a very bright area. Twelve recirculating "Water Farms" each hold one plant. A 20-inch fan recirculates the air. A 6-inch-diameter tube with fans at either end pulls hot air out of the garden to a remote window.

JAZZ'S GARDEN

This garden measures 3 feet by 12 feet, or 36 square feet. It is lit by two horizontally-mounted, 1000-watt, high-pressure sodium lamps. The lights are on a track, each moving a little less than six feet. The plants are being grown in a recirculating drip system using expanded clay pellets. The garden has evolved over several years and the yield is constantly rising as Jazz develops better growing methods and acquires better yielding varieties.

Ventilation is a problem because there is no direct air outlet. Jazz has installed a six-inch diameter air tube with a fan at either end that pushes and pulls the air in and out of the room.

Jazz's garden is productive. In addition to the high intensity light—over 55 watts per square foot—Jazz uses CO_2 to enhance growth rates. The walls are covered with Mylar. Harvests yield about two pounds of high-quality bud.

Smaller buds result from excessive branching

GROWING IN

The voters in 11 states have passed initiatives that allow medical patients or their caregivers to grow medicinal marijuana. You would think that politicians would get the hint and create realistic regulations to implement the new laws.

THE LIMITS
maximizing legal yields

THE PROBLEM IS THAT the criminal justice systems in the U.S. collectively spend $30 billion a year on prohibition and that represents a lot of jobs: from cops to DAs to judges to jailors to probation officers. In fact it's five percent of the national criminal justice budget. So we have the tail (cop) wagging the dog (politician). Hopefully, we will soon clip the dog's tail and train it to heel and stay. In the meantime we have to deal with the whims and vagaries of each jurisdiction's interpretation of the law. In California each county and city has its own regulations.

Two factors are usually considered in setting regulations for medical gardens. They are the canopy size and the number of plants. Sometimes a combination of these two is used to set guidelines. A few jurisdictions regulate by other factors, such as the number or wattage of lights; some have different rules for indoor and outdoor plants. In this chapter we will concentrate on plant numbers and canopy size.

There are techniques that can be used to maximize a garden's yield no matter what regulations are in force.

One is to purchase clones for use if they are available. It makes sense to use them rather than to root cuttings or start from seeds. When freed from producing starter plants, the gardener can devote more space to flowering plants or keep more plants in flowering. Even when there are provisions for

juvenile plants, it is still more efficient to bring rooted clones to the garden rather than home growing them.

This plant was grown in a 25-gallon container to encourage growth of a large root system that can support the vigorous growth of a large top canopy. The plant has grown large enough to capture most of the light emitted by the 1000-watt HPS lamp hung just above it.

Above: This room holds six home-constructed 1-cubic-yard boxes constructed from plywood. The garden is located in a jurisdiction that allows 6 plants, but has no size limit. Each box holds one plant. Each box is lit by its own 1000-watt lamp.

Plant Numbers

Plant number limits currently vary from a minimum of three to no limit. Between these two extremes, six plants is a popular regulatory number. A few jurisdictions distinguish between vegetative and flowering plants and allow a certain number of each.

Maximizing the yield within plant number limits means growing big plants that produce big yields. Plants are grown vegetatively for several months, until the canopy is large enough to capture all the light from a 400-watt or 1000-watt lamp. A 400-watt horizontal lamp with reflector covers approximately 2' x 3'. A 1000-watt lamp covers about 16 square feet. Using the techniques outlined below, a six plant garden could be lit by six lights.

I recommend growing plants in large containers, large hydroponic units or grow beds, so the roots have room to spread out. During the vegetative stage, feed them high-nitrogen formulas to promote growth. Some varieties naturally bush and need no pruning. Others can be encouraged to spread out by pinching the tops and training them. Each time the tip of the branch is removed or pinched, two branches grow in its place. These branches are then trained by pulling them down using string or weights. As the branches grow after being pulled down, they branch out like main branches, filling the canopy and capturing most of the light. Then the plant is ready to force to flower.

Another method of filling the canopy with low plant numbers is to grow plants until they are about 3 feet tall

Branches are tied down to encourage more extensive branching and to spread the plant out so all the light is captured.

and then turn them on their sides. In a few days the side branches will all start growing upwards as if they were main branches. To do this, the roots must be adapted to horizontal mode. First carefully remove the plant from its pot. Turn the container on its side and saw a new top hole. On the opposite side, create drainage holes. Since the container is cylindrical, it tends to roll. Wooden wedges or supports can be glued or taped to the container to keep it steady, or it can be placed in a frame. Replace the plant in the container in the same way that it was in the container before, but turn the container on its side with the newly cut hole facing up. The plant will now be watered through the hole you cut.

The plant will briefly be horizontal, but the branches will reorient themselves to grow upwards and these branches, now acting like main branches, will grow more side branching. After turning the container, the bottom half of the open end where the plant comes out must be blocked. A piece of plastic cut to size can be taped on using high quality duct tape.

Outdoors, it is not difficult to grow tall plants with girth. Choose large growing varieties adapted to the area. Grow the plants vegetatively indoors under 16 hours of light per day rather than under continuous light; otherwise they may flower immediately when they are moved outside. To grow quickly once outdoors, they need plenty of moisture and fertilizer, and full sun all day.

REGENERATION

Regeneration is a technique that can be used to speed up the vegetative growth stage. Once the flowers ripen, gardeners usually pull the plants and replace them with new ones. Instead of throwing plants away after harvesting, they are forced back into vegetative growth and then re-flowered.

This technique saves considerable time and labor. It is especially useful when growing a small number of large plants. By regenerating the plants instead of throwing them away, gardeners retain the root and branch infrastructure that it took so long to grow, so the vegetative growth stage is shortened. Plants can be regenerated a number of times. See the article on regeneration in this book for more information on this process.

Left: This collective outdoor garden was grown using home-constructed boxes. The jurisdiction has a plant number limit, but no size restriction. Each box holds ten plants, one patient's allocation. This setup was not only attractive, but it also made reaching the plants easy.

Left: This garden meets local regulations that call for no more than 35 plants in a maximum area of 32 square feet. Thirty-two five-gallon containers fit into the space. The plants need grow only a foot of canopy before they are forced to flower. The gardener can purchase clones at a local dispensary so he devotes the space only to flowering, not propagation.

Below:This garden was grown in a jurisdiction that limits space but has no plant limit. The plants are being grown in 6-inch-square containers. The 3' x 3' tray contains 24 containers, each with a single plant. Stakes support the stems so the buds stay in their allotted area, giving all of the buds access to light. This garden is a very efficient sea-of-green system.

Canopy Size

In areas where there are no plant limits there are usually canopy limits. Many small plants take less time to fill the canopy because they spend less time in vegetative growth—one to two weeks after seedlings or clones are transplanted, rather than three to six weeks spent growing plants to a larger size. This reduces the overall cycle by one to six weeks.

Another advantage of reducing the length of the vegetative stage is that it saves on energy. During vegetation, lights are on 18-24 hours a day. During flowering, they are only on 12 hours a day. The time savings in vegetative growth can reduce electrical usage by a third or more.

Two common canopy size limits are 32 square feet and 100 square feet. The typical 32 square foot garden is 4' x 8'. Usually gardeners place two 1000-watt lamps over the garden. However, if garden size is the limiting factor then additional light might be considered. Another 1000-watt lamp would increase light levels by 50%. Growth rate and yield both increase in a direct ratio to the increase in light as long as other factors, such as `water, nutrients, CO2 and temperature do not limit growth. Light increases temperature, so controlling the heat generated by additional light must be accounted for. Air-cooled reflectors provide one of the simplest solutions.

Canopy Size & Plant Number

When both canopy size and plant number are regulated, there is more of a challenge. Indoors, the quickest and most efficient way to create a full canopy regardless of garden size is to grow as many plants as are allowed. In outdoor gardens, where there is only a single harvest, the garden can either be many small plants or a few larger plants.

Indoors, strategic planning can be used to maximize production. For instance, in a jurisdiction that allows a maximum of 25 plants in 100 square feet, the plants should be divided between a 4' x 8' vegetative table and an 8' x 8' flowering table. Twelve plants are grown on each table. The vegetative table is lit by two 1000-watt lamps; the large flowering table is lit by four 1000-watt lamps. The plants will fill the canopy in about a week, and then the light regimen is changed to force them to flower.

One way of increasing the outdoor yield is to produce more than one harvest a year. Plants can be placed outdoors under cloches or in a greenhouse early in the season. Then, when they reach the desired size, they are blacked out for 12 hours each day using white/black plastic. In two months the plants will be ripe. These buds will be very potent because of the intense light they receive in midsummer. After the harvest the plants are replaced by a new group of starter plants. They will flower at the normal time.

Greenhouse growers and gardeners in the southern tier can grow all year long. In the north, natural light will have to be supplemented during the winter to support vigorous growth. To prevent flowering before the plants have grown to size, the long nights must be interrupted with light in the middle of the dark cycle. When the nighttime light is eliminated, the plants flower.

This outdoor garden contains only 6 very big plants. They cover an area of about 20' x 30'.

GENDER

There are several reasons why a grower would want a female marijuana plant to develop male flowers. Female pollen includes two X chromosomes, and no Y (the chromosome that makes plants male). All flowers fertilized by male flower pollen produced on a female plant will produce all-female seed.

BENDING
making males

THE CONVENIENCE OF planting a crop using all-female seed is obvious. The chore of sexing plants and the risk of pollination from a rogue male plant are eliminated. Rather than using clones, gardeners have the convenience of planting an all-female garden without clones.

Just think how much more peaceful a garden would be without the unwanted pollen created by stray males. In Holland I met a fellow who grew large amounts in a greenhouse. He said that the way he spotted males was by standing on a tower and looking at the garden with binoculars. If a plant was turning male or hermaphroditic, the surrounding females would all turn to face it. By the time that happened, it was often too late; some of the buds had been pollinated.

One male can spoil a good thing. They just have no respect for a grower's sinsemilla desires. What every grower needs is the peacefulness and tranquility of an all-female society, where there are no unplanned "events." Seeds from female-to-female crosses have absolutely no maleness in them to spoil a good season.

With female-to-female breeding, growers can choose the best females. They don't have to select a male. This is usually difficult because many of the characteristics being selected for are much more pronounced in the female. With a reliable way of inducing male flowers on a female, a breeder never has to face that dilemma. The best females can be selected without male intermediaries.

There are some problems using all-female crosses. Some varieties are more affected by artificial techniques that induce hermaphroditism. These plants respond more strongly to these methods, producing more male flowers than other types. Such plants may be more likely to carry genes promoting natural hermaphroditism than plants producing less pollen. A breeder may inadvertently be selecting for hermaphroditism when using pollen from a plant with copious production. This will not be apparent in the first few generations, but increased hermaphroditism may appear after four to six consecutive all-female crosses.

For this reason, it is best to limit the use of male pollen from female plants in breeding programs to only a few generations. However, this technique can be used to protect a plant's genetics without maintaining continuous cultivation. It can also be used to cross two particular plants without male intermediaries.

Above: Close-up of control. Inset: This variety showed some resistance to treatment. It produced only a few male flowers.

Top: Close-up of sprayed plant. Inset: Close-up of plant with both male and female flowers. The pollen from the flowers can be collected and used to fertilize either a non-sprayed version of the same plant or another desirable female.

The best use for feminized seed remains at the cultivation level. Two great females from different inbred lines can be crossed to create a hybrid in which the plants are quite uniform. If you aren't interested in uniformity, but in growing plants with diverse characteristics, cross two hybrid plants. With the genetic input from four different lines, the progeny will not be uniform, but will exhibit various qualities from each of its grandparents. Each plant will be unique. All of the plants will be female. The first generations have little more likelihood of natural hermaphroditism than the general population.

Gibberellic Acid

Gibberellic acid, a plant hormone, can be used to induce male flowering. However, most gardeners trying it have been disappointed. They reported stretched plants with running female flowers, but no males. However, induction of males using gibberellic acid has been reported in the scientific literature.

I decided to try an experiment to see whether there was a way of inducing male flowers in female plants using gibberellic acid. I used potassium gibberelate (.006 by weight, or 600 parts per million) in a spray form. Using several

varieties of plants including Dutch hybrids, the spray was applied as a light mist on the leaves of plants in various stages of development. When it was sprayed on flowering plants or plants about to be placed in flowering, the spray resulted in running buds—that is, sparse buds with wide gaps between individual flowers.

> **"With female-to-female breeding, growers can choose the best females. They don't have to select a male."**

The experiment was performed on clones cut from known female clone mothers that were rooted and in vegetative growth. It was only when the plant or plant part was sprayed two weeks before inducing flowering and again at induction of forcing (by increasing the dark regimen from 0 to 12 hours daily), that male flowers were produced. All of the plants under this regimen exhibited male flowering. We also found that the effect is localized—only the sprayed areas are affected.

The pollen produced on male flowers induced with gibberellic acid is fertile. It has been used to produce seeds with

female flowers on the same plant as well as with other plants. The seeds were germinated and produced normal female plants but no males.

The acclaimed American-Dutch breeder, Soma, was not the first person to notice that some buds produce male flowers just as they ripen. If buds are left to over-ripen, they produce even more flowers with viable pollen. The flowers are being produced by the female plant as part of its last ditch strategy to reproduce. The flowers have only female chromosomes so all of their progeny will be female. This pollen can be collected and used to produce feminized seed. Soma was the first to use the technique of collecting this pollen to create feminized seed.

There are reports of using other methods to induce male flowers in female plants. Some growers report that aspirin dissolved in the water results in male flowers. Irregular light cycles during flowering also sometimes results in hermaphroditism, but there is no research on how to develop hermaphrodites consistently using either of these methods.

JAKE: GARDENING

Jake has an interesting story to tell. Without describing his circumstances too much I can tell you that he has seen the world from both perspectives because he has been up, faced disaster and pulled himself up again. His strong character has allowed him to persevere in the face of daunting odds and negative prognostications. These are Jake's thoughts about gardening and life.

VETERAN
inside his garden

MY CLASS'S PROPHECY of what I would be doing 20 years after high school was that I would marry a fox, move to Mexico and grow my own crops. The year I graduated, my friends and I planted 1,000 unsexed plants in gallon containers on a 35-acre plot surrounded by corn. That was before airplanes and before sexing. We harvested in October using machetes and saws. My first crop was very seedy product. Its heritage was a mix of Colombian and Mexican stash seed.

We planted the next year but the airplanes came and took it all away, so I moved out of state, then joined the army, went to Germany and didn't grow for five years. When I returned to civilian life, I kept plants in 20" containers that held 2.5 cubic feet of soilless mix. I was in the desert, so I moved them in and out of the garage to protect against the cold night air. They loved the sun, though. Using the garage to regulate light allowed me to harvest throughout the growing season and throughout the winter. By that time I'd learned about sinsemilla.

After two years, I moved back home and grew a small indoor garden. I had one 1000-watt high-pressure sodium lamp over a 25-square-foot garden. It was a hydro garden with plants growing out of a container filled with clay pebbles in an aerated solution that was kept light-free. That continued for 10 years. This garden was in perpetual harvest and was very productive, generating about 12 ounces a month. It had seven trays that each held four plants. I had a number of varieties that took varying times to mature, so I

replaced them with new plants as they were harvested. About two plants a week were felled with a pair of snippers with sharp blades. They were immediately replaced with rooted plants grown in a separate area under a 400-watt metal halide lamp. They were 15 inches tall and somewhat bushy when they were forced. The tops were often cut from them to use as clone material. Other cuts were also made to root for future crops.

After I stopped doing that, I moved north and got back to my professional business for a while. However, I must have been under bad influences, or perhaps a bad element, or maybe I'm just an addictive personality. I just couldn't stay away from growing. I tried, but it's hard, and I succumbed.

I had this friend who hangs around with a lot of characters. So when I was staying at his house I met this fellow who visited frequently. He seemed nice enough, and it turned out that he was growing outdoors in a rural part of northern California. He was also involved in making candies, and he drew me into that circle. Before I knew it, I was spending less time on doing my "professional" work and more time hanging out watching the confections go by.

Then my friend suggested that we grow together. Well, I might have suggested it. I don't remember. But whoever suggested it, it didn't take much for the other to agree. We decided to grow in San Francisco because of the acceptance and tolerance by the government of the City and County of San Francisco.

We found a real estate agent and told him we were going to run a production studio. I didn't specify what kind, but I think he thought we were involved with video or something. We chose the space because it looks smaller than it really is. It was already zoned commercial and was wired for industrial use, so we have never had to worry about pulling too much power. When we moved in, it was one big space: 45' x 30' with 10' ceilings. We built two flowering rooms, each 32' long and 11' wide. Each of the rows is 4' wide with a 3' center aisle. Each row is lit by eight 600-watt HPS lamps.

There were no ventilation systems in the space except, of course, for the five-ton air conditioner. This has come in really handy, and we use it 24-7. We built the ventilation system using it. Each room has two 6" and one 10" duct blowing cool air from the AC. The rooms are each exhausted by an 8" and a 10" Excel Inline fan made by Fantek. Both are equipped with charcoal filters. To circulate the air in the room we have five 18" King-Air wall-mount fans.

It seemed that rockwool would be the easiest way to maintain the garden, even though it would take a little more time to set up. We wound up using 4" rockwool cubes slapped onto 8" wide slabs—four per 40' slab. We use eight slabs per 4' x 8' black plastic tray. The slabs are irrigated every other day using an ebb and flow system. There are 4 trays on each side of the room.

Each side of the room has its own irrigation system. There are four 150-gal-lon reservoirs holding solution outside of the room. We have been using General Hydroponics as recommended and tweak it with Superthrive, Cal-Mag by Bionicare and Protek. We change the reservoir every eight days, after about four irrigations. Once we make the solution, we don't add water to it or adjust it. We use up about 85% of the water.

After the fourth irrigation, we dump any solution that's left and add clear water. In San Francisco our water is almost mineral-free and has a pH near 7, so we just adjust the pH to 6 and let it flow. It dissolves the fertilizer salts in the rockwool and gets it ready for a new fertilizer formula. After that we add new fertilizer and start over.

We foliar feed with Nitrozyme weekly for the first 6 weeks of flowering. This seaweed fertilizer greens up the plants and seems to make them more vigorous and increases their growth. Every second week we spray them with an iron-zinc chelated spray. Then once a week we spray with Organicide as a preventative against mites and insects.

We flower the plants for about 10 weeks. This is longer than the "ripening time" suggested for most of the varieties, but I find that the buds are much denser, tastier and frostier than harvesting after eight weeks, as recommended.

This garden is a valuable service to the community. I serve a lot of AIDS patients who get their medicine for free or at very reduced rates. This medicine helps keep them alive and

Lights are put on movers to get more coverage.

Left: Day and nighttime temperatures and humidity levels are kept in check.
Right: pH and ppm meters keep a constant eye on the situation.

healthy. We know that many of our patients have damaged immune systems, so we take care not to trigger any reactions. We strive to take exceptional care regarding hygiene. We sweep and mop every day and we're pesticide free.

We use a combination of sesame seed oil and fish oil mixed in water to prevent insect infections, which I read about in a little garden store in the middle of nowhere. They had it on the shelf, and I bought a bottle of it. I had been battling mites that had gotten out of control. This worked at knocking them off. We spray it underneath the leaves up to the seventh week of flowering. We use a pump sprayer because power sprayers have too much power, and the oil would end up on the bud, making them crispy but not appetizing.

Once you bond with marijuana you have a desire to plant more and watch it grow. One of the favorite things I like to do in my garden is smoke a big fat joint from the mama of the babies that are growing in the room. I made a lot more money running my own computer company, but I never experienced the joy I feel working in the garden every day. It's made me more tolerant, and more importantly, it's made me more generous in sharing and caring.

When I was 16 years old, a veteran smoker of three years, cannabis went from being a vice to a habit, an every-

day thing. My class prophecy, that I would move to Mexico to grow pot never came true, but it has been an important part of my life. I might not have made it to Mexico, but I ended up growing crops. I guess they were half right.

Life without pot would be rather boring. I wouldn't be as mellow and I'd be more impatient, stressed and high strung. Life wouldn't be as enjoyable. I'd miss the creativity and the good times hanging with my friends smoking it. Working with the plants is a meditation on trying to take good care of them and figuring how to improve their growth and their environment. It takes me into another realm. It's been very influential and insightful.

IN JAKE'S GARDEN

I GROW FOUR VARIETIES:

Ice, which is predominantly red-haired skunk. It has a lot of sativa qualities and naturally needs a longer ripening time.

Romulan, which is some of the best pot I have ever smoked. It is very effective for arthritis and excellent for pain management. AIDS patients like it because it stops their nausea. Recreational users say that its hybrid qualities, about 50-50 sativa/indica, leads to an especially intense high. It's easy to grow, very hardy and ripens in about 9.5 weeks.

Triple X is an indica plant that people use to regulate their sleep. It's heavily intoxicating, with almost a narcotic high. Its taste is a combination of fruitiness and a dry champagne that expands in your lungs. First hits usually result in tubercular–like coughs. It is fully ripe at 10 weeks—the glands all swollen and glistening in the light. At 10 weeks they shout, "Pick me! Pick me!" as I walk through their section. They let me know when they are ready.

Pez is an indica that is very popular among people who vaporize. It has a smooth inhale, almost like you're drinking water. It doesn't make you cough. It seems to help with pain. However, it is a very low yielder. It develops a purple color as it comes into full ripening at nine weeks, not the seven recommended. Most people who grow it never see the purple color because they harvest too early.

ROOM FOR

The San Francisco/Bay Area has a burgeoning medical marijuana community. Some patients grow their own, but many have some interaction with the medical patient cooperatives. These centers may be the source of their supply of bud or of clones from which they start and maintain a garden with medical-quality plants. Co-operatives are mostly supplied by large-scale growers, who use twenty or more lights.

IMPROVEMENT
extreme garden makeover

THE FOLLOWING IS THE STORY of one co-op supplier and his garden. An acquaintance told me that he had a big space which could be used as a grow. He had made arrangements with the landlord and we agreed to invest in the 10,000 square foot space together. I had years of experience growing and I thought this space would be perfect. It had good ventilation that was left from the last tenant. The space had been used as a sewing factory. All the electricity and fans were in place. The space needed only minor modifications to make two giant rooms for flowering.

We used wood framing and black/white plastic polyethylene to create the spaces. Each room holds three 10' x 20' pods with 2-foot walkways between them. The pods were made using 2' x 4's placed on the floor. They were lined with 30-ml butyl rubber, the same kind used for fish ponds, so they are totally waterproof.

I've tried a wide range of growing methods. After experimenting with drip, constant flow and flood systems I went back to planting mix in containers because I think it is the most convenient method of growing. The containers are placed on slats to allow for drainage. Each pod holds 392 2-gallon containers. It does take some work at the planting stage, but it is very easy to care for and very forgiving. I have tried all kinds of soils too. I tried the least expensive house brands and most expensive brands such as JR but I found the most inexpensive high quality soil is Black Gold®.

I add only water while the plants are in growth stage, maturing from clones to young ladies. At three weeks I prune the plants and take cuttings. The plants are about 15-18 inches tall then. I cut the growing tip and leave the four healthiest branches, which are staked. I use the branches I removed for cuttings and put up clones using Oasis 1015's. This is a synthetic material that wicks water and is sterile. A 10" x 20" nursery tray holds 50 cubes.

After a few days of adjusting to their trimmed state and the loss of the primary growing tip, the light is changed from constant to 12/12 and they are triggered into bloom. Then, I begin fertilizing them. I give them Old Age

> **"After experimenting with drip, constant flow and flood systems I went back to planting mix in containers because I think it is the most convenient method of growing."**

Each room holds three 10' x 20' pods. The yellow card hanging from the front light is a sticky indicator trap for aphids and fungus gnats. The ballasts mounted along the back wall generate unneeded heat. The reflectors, designed for air cooling, are not being used with an air-cooling set-up so they are also releasing heat. Lights are placed about 3 feet above the plant canopy so the light gets dispersed evenly.

This young plant was located in a heat-stress area. Note the droopy leaves, tissue necrosis and limited growth.

Organic Growth Formula once a week as directed. I water daily, alternating with liquid kelp or bat guano rated at 3-10-1. Once in a while I skip a day of watering and I occasionally skip a day of fertilizing.

Each room has four 40-gallon reservoirs, one at each end of a walkway. The water is plumbed to the reservoirs. We use little pumps to keep the water circulating. This keeps the fertilizer mixed and adds oxygen to the water. We pump water through a 25-foot hose to hand water the plants. A reservoir holds enough water to fill a pod so three reservoirs are used in the room each day.

To keep the humidity down, two huge dehumidifiers condense the moisture. I use forced air (fans blowing air into the room) to maintain positive air pressure. Since the air pressure is higher inside the room than it is outside, air is constantly pushing out of the room through small vents as well as through cracks and crevices. This makes it harder for insects and pests to enter the space.

The rooms are set up with CO2 using tanks. An online monitor controls the rate of injection. I try to keep the CO2

at about 1200 parts per million. Rotating fans mounted on the walls gently blow air on the plants. Larger fans blow air toward the ceiling.

Less water is required when the plants go into bloom because the lights are off half the time. After the second week of flowering, I change the fertilizer to Old Age Organic Bloom. At this time straggly branches and new adventitious growth are trimmed off. Then we just baby-sit the plants for another four weeks until the buds ripen.

We monitor constantly for insects and plant pests. We remove big shade or fan leaves to allow the light to get directly to the bud. I use nematodes and yellow (aphids and fungus gnats) and blue (thrips) pest traps for monitoring. However my main problem was spider mites. I never got rid of them but contained them with Safers Soap and neem oil. Mold has also been a problem. The mold grew when there was too much humidity and heat. Bringing in the dehumidifiers and positive air pressure eliminated the problem. I sprayed baking soda at one teaspoon per quart to control powdery mildew.

Each pod uses seven 600-watt lamps and three 1000s. The 1000s are in the center of the pod and use an umbrella reflector so that the light spreads out over the entire garden. The seven 600s pick up a lot of shade so that all areas have light. The ballasts are hung high on the wall. Unfortunately, they contribute to a lot of heat to the room. If I

> "I tried the least expensive house brands and expensive brands such as JR but I found the most inexpensive high quality soil is Black Gold. "

Part of the garden located near a stream of cool air. The plants are growing faster, look healthier and are not ripening prematurely. The moderate light levels will limit the bud size and density.

had it to do over again, I'd move them to the other side of the wall.

Heat is a concern. All the reflectors, except the umbrella shades, could be connected up to vent out the air. Each time a garden is created you learn how to make it better. At one time I thought this was the ultimate garden but now I see its shortcomings. It really needs air conditioning.

I use two deodorizing tubs filled with deodorizing gel. I supercharged its action by having a fan blow over it. I like the gels because they don't mask the odor, but eliminate it. I use an ozone generator by the front door.

"Then we just baby-sit the plants for another four weeks until the buds ripen. "

Top: Clones were still being planted in the flowering room. These plants are about 10 inches tall. They won't get a chance to grow vegetatively before they are flowered, but will be grown as single stem plants. Inset: Garden suffering from heat stress: limp leaves, slowed growth, low yield.

Right: This branch, four weeks into flowering, has a small bud which is ripening prematurely from heat stress. Inset: A healthy plant one week into flowering. This plant was located near a vent and received a constant stream of cool air.

My partner knew a fellow with a unique strain called Coral Reef. The grower was reluctant to share the variety but we promised not to sell the clones, especially to the medical co-ops. We bought 1000 plants at $20 apiece. I had 28 varieties at one time. I bought the clones at the co-ops and then propagated them. We liked the Max 49 and J27 and the Champagne. These are very popular at the medical co-ops. I dumped a lot of plants I should probably have kept, but after a while I got tired of them. I let the G-13 and Cali-O go, for instance. They're still around so I guess I could get them back.

> "Each time a garden is created you learn how to make it better."

To keep the area cool, the lights are on at night from 7 pm to 7 am. Here in the East Bay, the temp cools 20 degrees at night. The lights were rewired to 240 volts. This lowers the use of electricity and the bill by one third. The light becomes a lot more efficient.

The perimeter is secured with rolls of razor wire inconspicuously hidden in shafts and crawl spaces. The front has a roll back top. Employees working at night while the lights are on also discourages burglaries. The space is closed during the day.

We cut down all the plants in a pod after seven weeks when the Coral Reef is fully mature. We have a drying room with a dehumidifier. We dry the plants on racks made with screenings. We dry the leaves for making hash and hash oil. Then we trim the leaf off the bud. We don't process it but other people in the area specialize in processing. All the bud goes to the co-ops for medical use."

Four weeks into flowering, the plants show signs of heat stress: lanky growth with stretched buds. The moderately low light levels also produce stretched, small buds.

1. Open the doors to the hallway and let some of the hot air out of the room and some of the cool ventilated workroom air in.

2. Turn off the fans blowing air down from the roof. Instead, let the hot air rise out of the garden.

3. There is a cork tile false ceiling hiding a 14-foot ceiling. Remove some of the ceiling boards so the hot air can rise.

4. Turn on the roof ventilating fans to pull the hot air from the top of the room.

5. The twenty-one 600-watt lamps in each room are designed so they can be used as air-cooled reflectors. Set up the air-cooled option by attaching portable ducting to the lamps with fans blowing air in and out. With air-cooled lights, most of the lamps' heat never gets into the room. Cool air is drawn into the tubing and is heated as it passes through the lights. The ducting exhausts outside the grow room.

6. Move the ballasts out of the grow rooms to a space where they can be kept cool. This would eliminate thousands of BTUs of heat from the space.

7. Install a ventilation system drawing air from the back of the building to each of the grow rooms. The cool night air should be filtered before it enters the room. Excess air will be drawn out by the roof fans.

This garden has produced well before, during the winter and spring, it's just that during the warmer weather there is no way to deal with the heat. By using some of these techniques, the temperature could be controlled and the plants saved from stress.

After telling me his tale, he asked if I would like to see the garden. We made arrangements to meet a few days later.

I parked the car on a commercial street and rang the bell, staring at the corrugated metal of the roll-up doors. My host opened a side door and ushered me in to the space. We walked through a reception area to a work/storage space. The doors to the flowering rooms were in this area. The mother plants and clones were usually upstairs, but the area was being remodeled. One room had been placed in flowering about a week before, although young plants were still being stuffed into the space as they were potted. The other room was forced about four weeks before.

As soon as the door to the first flowering room was opened, a wave of heat hit me. The work area was a cool 70 degrees, 10 degrees warmer than the cool East Bay evening. The flowering room, with twenty-one 600-watt lamps and nine 1000s in total was 80 to 100 degrees depending on the spot. The 21 kilowatts+ was making the room too hot and there was not enough ventilation for it to be evacuated. The hotter areas had stressed plants, but the plants in the cooler areas were growing well.

The 200-square-foot pods were each lit by 7200 watts of electrical input, an average of only 36 watts per square foot. The plants would have produced larger buds under 60 watts psf. Each pod could use another 3,000 watts. This would give the plants the energy to produce thick, resin-coated buds.

I looked around. With a few hours of effort and not too much investment, this space could be turned around.

HARVEST

A successful outdoor harvest depends on planning the garden so that the weather and plants conspire to produce completely mature buds. Outdoors, bud growth is subject to the vagaries of the weather. The bud's size, development and ripening time are all dependent on the environment. Warm weather with full sun hastens growth and ripening. Cool, cloudy weather slows growth because the plant is receiving less light, which fuels growth. Moist, cloudy or rainy weather is a threat to the developing bud because it encourages the growth of fungi and molds. A season's effort can be spoiled in hours if mold develops— white or gray molds can turn beautiful buds to mush or cause them to become brown and crumble when touched. This is one reason why all farmers are throwing the dice each time they plant. Of course, tomato farmers don't have the additional worries about thieves or the boys in blue.

PROBLEM SOLVING
coping with nature

NO MATTER HOW BIG the plants are, the initiation of flowering and the date of maturity are both determined by the critical dark period, the number of hours of darkness that triggers and sustains flowering. Any interruption of the dark period results in delayed flowering and may affect the buds' growth patterns, making them lanky. Plants use red light to measure day length. This is mostly relevant to people in urban areas who might consider growing near a street or outdoor light. Plants growing outdoors near a street lamp or patio light will never fully enter the flowering phase.

While buds require a completely dark period to trigger flowering, the other portion of the daily cycle, the light period, triggers growth. Buds exposed to the most light grow larger and mature faster. Under an intense sun, marijuana buds grow fat and juicy. How ironic that they flower just as the sun's strength wanes in the fall. Buds grown in the shade don't reach their full potential. In very shady locations they may never fully mature. Every sunny day speeds the plant to maturity. Overcast days do nothing. The plant just sits there, in suspended animation, waiting for some ripening energy.

Left: The stigmas have dried and are receding into the calyxes. These are enlarging as if the plants were pollinated and were forming seed. Meanwhile, the glands are filling with THC.
Bottom: This bud is ripening but still has weeks to go before it has reached full potency. The glands are visible but not filled with the seductively intoxicating resin.

the bud has finished most of its growth. The major change will now be in appearance, from a young bud with thousands of tender stigmas vainly searching the air for pollen grains, to a mature bud.

The key change is in the stigmas and ovaries. At the start, the stigmas are a pale translucent color—white or cream, which is sometimes tinged pink or purple. They glow when they catch the light. As the bud continues to ripen, these structures begin to dry out. They will turn orange, red or purple by the time the bud is ripe. Then the ovaries

Plants in the southern U.S., which experience shorter days throughout the summer and fall than the northern U.S., mature earlier. Plants grown at high altitudes mature seven to ten days faster than those in the valley. Different varieties of marijuana also range in how long they require to mature. Equatorial sativas have been bred in climates that have a longer day and a more intense sun with less seasonal variation. The indicas or hybrids from temperate regions have thrived or been selected because they can mature before winter frost halts their progress. As a result, sativas tend to have a longer flowering time and indicas a shorter time. Many varieties are hybrids, and they may range in maturation time based on the genetics they've inherited from their parents.

The Drama of Ripening

On June 22, the first full day of summer, the sun turns course to shorten each day, and increase each night's length. As the nights grow longer each plant's critical dark period is reached, and the plants begin to flower. Flowering progresses with the coming of fall.

Anticipation of harvest starts about three weeks before the plants ripen. Stigmas have appeared along the nodes where the leaves meet the branches and the branches meet the stem. The pistils have grown enough to outline the future bud. The buds have entered the home stretch. Every day they are a little closer to ripeness, but are not quite there. Although a few more flowers will appear,

begin to swell. Soon the stigmas will recede partly inside as the ovaries take a bulbous shape.

Plants should be given time to ripen. When buds are first forming, resin glands that hold THC cover the surface, but they don't swell until the buds ripen. They grow taller structures and stand erect from the tissue in anticipation. Chemicals and enzymes are converted into THC on the inner surface of the membrane, which forms the top of the gland.

The glands start to fill out within weeks, turning into mushroom-shaped organs littering the leaves and stem, but especially the flowers. Then the bulb at the end inflates like a balloon, stretching more each day. The clear, intoxicating oil inside each gland glistens. In the noon sun, the glands become luminescent. They have a halo when the sun is behind them at the end of the day. They radiate electricity. Just looking at them, you get a shiver of energy going up your spine.

The plants are still putting out a few new flowers, but the colas are ripe and another generation of marijuana has grown to complete its life cycle. It is hard to believe that a few months ago these plants were just a few seeds in a bottle.

The plant's essence is captured in its extended colas—the long, resin-covered buds that shine like jewels against the floral background of autumn foliage. Twinkling in the breeze, the buds look like holy spirits dancing to the waning sun. Just as resin glands begin to change from clear to a slightly cloudy tan or brown, the magic moment has arrived, and the plants are ready to be harvested.

Using a photographer's loupe, you can get a better look at the bud and its glands. If the gland head membrane looks like it could be stretched, the bud still has a way to go before ripening. If the gland head membrane looks taut, like an overfilled balloon, the bud is probably ready. When the gland heads look clear, the THC is still accumulating. When they start to turn cloudy, the THC is deteriorating to cannabinol, which is only one-tenth as psychoactive as THC.

Guerilla Safety

The most important consideration when you are readying for harvest is safety. Guerilla gardens are often under police surveillance, and harvest is the most vulnerable phase of growing. The plants are at their largest size and their strongest fragrance. It is easier to suffer from reckless impatience or paranoia when the reward for your work is right around the corner. Once harvest begins, you are carrying budded plants on your person or possibly in your car. Therefore, it is best to make sure before going to the garden for harvesting that it won't yield an invitation to court. Police use motion or heat detectors, video cameras and stakeouts to trap gardeners. Motion detectors work day or night, but are ineffective in windy weather and rain. Heat detectors are not effective during the day. Video cameras record cultivators in the act so that they may be picked up later. They are ineffective after dark. A stakeout is the most dangerous because it consists of a bunch of gung-ho's playing cops and robbers. Police in this situation can be very dangerous.

Before going to the garden, check the surrounding perimeter to see if everything's okay. Take a walk during the day with your plant, rock or naturalist guide and a bag of newly collected stones or mosses. Since there is no connection between you and the garden, police will have no cause to detain you should you be stopped. On your walk around the

Top: Guerilla grower dumps his load of buds.

Second: A Wisconsin bud being trimmed.

Third: First the big fan leaves are removed. Once the fan leaves and large secondary leaves are removed, other excess leaves should be removed, leaving only the small bud leaves, which are also covered with glands. The bud should be covered but not hidden. If the bud is alone on a stick it should be removed, but there is no reason to separate large buds.

After trimming, the buds should be placed back into the curing room. After ten days the temperature of the room should be raised into the high 80's and air circulation continued so that the buds dry.

Bottom: In a garden of mixed varieties plants ripen at different times. This makes it easier for a small crew to harvest the plants. They can do it over 4 to 6 weeks rather than all at once.

perimeter, look for signs of cops, cameras or electronic equipment.

Getting to the Harvest

According to University of Mississippi studies, the best time to harvest is very early in the morning, just before dawn, when the plants are at their most potent. Serendipitously, very few police are on-duty, and the world is asleep.

Harvesting techniques must fit the circumstances. Ideally the plant can be harvested according to its natural progress to maturity. Most of the time, a plant's bottom buds ripen first, with the top buds reaching maturity as long as ten days later. In order to allow each bud to reach an absolutely perfect ripeness, the home gardener can pick the branches one-by-one as they finish. Outdoor gardeners rarely have ideal circumstances, and often face hard choices. The buds are a few sunny days from harvest, but the weather predictions are for rain and overcast days for the next week. Is it worth waiting out the rain until the next sunny morning? Or maybe neighbors' kids have already clipped a few immature buds from the plants. Who will harvest, the kids or you? Perhaps helicopters are active in the next valley. Should you harvest before the sightseers arrive? These are some hard questions with no clear answers except in hindsight. The stress of allowing near-perfect bud to remain vulnerable to weather, mold, thieves and the law may just not be worth it. A gardener may opt to harvest the entire plant at once. In this case, gardeners usually chop down the whole plant and clip the branches from the stem in the privacy of home.

If you have a lot of large plants to harvest and noise is not a problem, use a hedge trimmer. Starting at the top, clip all the branches in a straight cut to the bottom of the plant. The branches will fall into a very neat pile. Move on to the next line of branches and repeat the cut from top to bottom. Each plant has four lines of branches. After the branches are cut, line them up by the bud tips. You will find that the colas are about the same length. You can cut the bare part of the branches off right at the site. Plants can also be cut this way by a strong person with a sharp machete and a firm grip. For moderately sized plants, a high quality hand clipper is usually adequate.

This bud is ripe. The glands are filled and it sparkles like a monument studded with precious gems.

The glands are filled; the bud is ripe and ready to go.

Green Light for Safety

Gardeners who wish to examine their plants at night need to be concerned not only about safety, but about changing their plant's photo period. As 12 complete hours of darkness is imperative for proper flowering, even the dim light of a flashlight can return the plant to the vegetative state.

Most of a flashlight's light is in the yellow, orange and red spectra. Even fluorescent ones emit some red light. The solution is to place a green filter over the light source, as plants are not sensitive to this color. If you are gardening out in the woods at night, a green flashlight is an essential tool. It gives you sight, but is unobtrusive, hard to see from a distance, and blends into the background.

A green filter can easily be made from a stage-light filter, or, more conveniently, from four or five layers of green plastic from an appropriately sized pop bottle. Choose a size that slides over the flashlight top, but is not too loose. Cut the bottle about four inches from the bottom. Then cut four pieces from the side of the bottle. Slide the bottle bottom with the extra green pieces in it over the flashlight and tape it on.

Tips for Success

1.) Once the colas are removed from the plant, they are quite compact, and quite a few will fit in a flower box, even when they are two feet long.

2.) Whether you are harvesting from a garden, a field or a unique grow site, keep your exposure limited by spending as little time as possible harvesting and on the road with unprocessed plants.

3.) If the weather is turning nasty, remember that the plant is feeling it too. That is all the more reason for going out and harvesting rather than hanging out by the warm hearth or electric heater.

4.) Don't indulge while driving. Obey speed limits, lights and road signs. Drive cautiously.

5.) Make sure there are no ambiguous parts to the plan and that it is worked out in detail before you start traveling. If someone else is involved, make sure you agree on the plans and have the watches as well as time responsibilities synchronized.

Post-Harvest Tips on Curing and Storing

After the plants are harvested, they may be trimmed of large leaves and hung to dry in a cool, dark, drafty room for a few days to let the chlorophyll decompose and some of the starches turn to sugar. The draft, using both external ventilation and internal circulation fans, keeps mold from forming. The buds turn from a bright green to a dull green with tints of orange, red or purple in a few days. The temperature should be raised to 85°F, and airflow maintained until the buds are dry, but not crisp.

Then they are ready to be stored. The best storage method is in darkened glass or hard plastic (tupperware-type) containers that can be sealed. These should be kept in a cool place, including the refrigerator or freezer. A cool, dark environment sealed from air exposure reduces the degrading effects of light and oxidation. Glass or hard plastic containers are better than ziplock-type plastic bags. This is because plastic bags develop a static cling–like electric attraction. Glands get stuck by this attraction to the inside of the bag and are unrecoverable.

Top: These buds were brought indoors for manicuring and drying on a rack. It took ten days for them to reach perfection.

Left: These buds were hung on a line outdoors. They were manicured as they were drying. Some had already been clipped, while others were waiting patiently on line for their haircut.

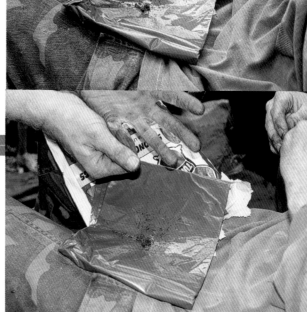

After manicuring for an hour, hands were sticky with resin. The resin was removed by rubbing the hands together. As it peeled from the hands it rolled up to form little cylinders. These were rolled up to make balls of finger hash.

THE FUTURE OF

For millennia cannabis has been involved in a symbiotic relationship with humans. It's an extremely adaptable plant and has traveled all over the world with them. It grows on the cold steppes of Russia, in equatorial climates and in the last forty years, has found a home indoors.

MARIJUANA BREEDING
designing tomorrow's varieties

BY THE TIME late twentieth century breeders started manipulating marijuana's genes, there were thousands of cultivated varieties to work with. In addition, there were hundreds of landraces to choose from.

The first marijuana varieties cultivated in the U.S. by the new breeders were Sativas, including Colombian, Jamaican and Mexican. These plants were tall and lanky and matured in mid-October through November. The fresh material was far superior to the degraded bricked buds from which it emerged.

These Sativas were unsuitable for indoor cultivation because they grew too vigorously; they were too tall and produced long thin buds. After a long flowering period they produced small yields.

Trekkers returned from Afghanistan, India and other Himalayan regions with new genetics: the Indicas. These plants were compact and shorter than Sativas; they also had a shorter flowering period and were heavier yielders.

Jingles, a Northern California grower and breeder, invented Skunk #1 with a fortuitous cross between a stabilized Mexican Acapulco Gold x Afghani hybrid and a Colombian Gold plant. Skunk #1 is very adaptable and originally ripened in 8 to 10 weeks, or outdoors in mid-October in Central California. Later versions, including the one that arrived in Holland, ripened more quickly.

Apocryphally, the famed Haze Brothers developed Haze from crosses of two hybrids. The first was an Acapulco Gold x Colombian Gold cross, perhaps the same one or a cousin of the one used by Jingles. The second was a South Indian x Thai stabilized hybrid adapted to central California. This variety also arrived in Holland by the mid-1970s.

Two other varieties played major roles in the modern domestication of marijuana. Northern Lights was supposedly developed in a government lab in the state of Washington. This story may be an urban myth; nevertheless, it did originate in the U.S. Northwest. This plant was a hybrid that produced both Sativa-like and Indica-like progeny, most notably NL1 and NL5. These plants were used in crosses developed by famed seed breeder Nevil Schumacher when he was proprietor of the Seed Bank. The Indica version had a very short flowering time and was bountiful. When crossed with Haze to produce NL5-Haze, it was easily the most potent plant available for many years.

A mixed garden showing some variations of large plants grown to fit within the plant limits.

Left foreground- a vigorous Indica-Sativa hybrid.
Right foreground- The creeper. To keep it off the ground, it was planted in a planter made of two truck tires. The branches are about to grow along the ground.
Left middle and right back- Giant Sativas. The other plants are hybrids. This garden is about 15' x 40' and contains just seven plants, the legal limit in Oregon.

White Widow was the last plant to join the foursome of progenitor plants commonly used in breeding programs. It was developed by Ingmar of the defunct Master Seed Company, who provided it to several major Dutch breeders. It is reputedly a backcross of a Brazilian with a South Indian. I doubt the South Indian heritage because Indicas are found in the northern areas of India near the Himalayas, not in the south. Regardless, it is an Indica-Sativa cross that has a short flowering time of 60 to 70 days and is very potent. It is an excellent substitute for Skunk #1 because it shows more of its Indica lineage. The first introductions to the public had not been stabilized and varied when reproduced, but later versions, including many available today, were inbred for uniformity.

Most marijuana grown in Europe and North America probably has one or more of these varieties in its ancestry. Except for Haze, these varieties had controlled growth as compared with the landraces from which they originated. They were also very fast maturing plants, ripening in October rather than November outdoors, and within 75 days inside. These characteristics revolutionized growing. Gardeners could harvest four crops a year with a yield of a pound or more per 1000-watt lamp rather than two or three crops with one-half to three-quarter pound yields.

Other strains were added to the breeding mix. They included the fast maturing South African Sativas, Brazilians, Thais and Southeast Asian varieties. All lent novel characteristics to the mix.

The three characteristics that breeders have been most interested in are potency, ripening time and growth pattern. Although there were always very potent varieties, tests showed the best varieties reaching the high teens and even 20% THC content for the first time in the mid-1990s. At the same time there are more potent varieties to choose from so the general level of cannabis available is more potent today than ever.

Other factors that breeders consider but which are of less concern are aroma and taste and the look of the bud. However, aroma and taste are loosely associated with potency and the cosmetic look with yield, so these characteristics improve as potency and yield increases.

Potency

In contrast to today's marijuana, the imported varieties of yesteryear were quite mild. Mexican usually had a potency of 2% to 6% and even the Colombians were mostly under 10%. Even the Thai exotics that old-timers reminisce about would be considered only moderately strong.

As the potency increased, breeders became more concerned about the quality of the high. A look at any variety profile provides a description of the high. One enthusiast, Masaya in Yokohama, Japan, after considerable contemplation, divided the high into 27 mental states.

From this list it is apparent that the cannabinoids have the potential to affect people in many different ways. Current breeding is mostly centered on the effects of the cannabinoids. Breeders consider both the effects on the brain; that is, how it affects your mental outlook, and its medical properties for a host of diseases and conditions.

In the 1990s Dave Watson's Dutch company, Hortifarm, developed a number of varieties of marijuana that each produced primarily one cannabinoid, so the effects of each cannabinoid or of various combinations could be ascertained relatively easily. GW Pharmaceuticals used these patented varieties to develop their natural cannabinoid spray for relief of multiple sclerosis symptoms. The spray contains equal amounts of THC and CBD. Hortifarm's plants included strains that produced spikes around the cannabinoids CBN and CBL, so we may expect to see some medicines built around these cannabinoids as well.

Commercial breeders are beginning to use equipment to test for cannabinoid

An Alien Trainwreck cola.

Close-up of immature flowers of the sativa hybrid. They are somewhat denser than typical sativa flowers.

content. This will be a valuable tool in developing varieties with specific qualities. In the San Francisco Bay Area, there are more than thirty legal medical marijuana dispensaries that offer medicine to patients who hold a doctor's recommendation. Many of the centers offer specific types of marijuana for various problems. The person using marijuana for post-traumatic stress will probably use a different variety than the person seeking relief from the side effects of chemotherapy.

Have you ever noticed how fresh marijuana that still retains a strong odor will have subtly different effects when it is stale? The odor causing molecules are called mono- and di-terpenes. They are similar to essential oils but they have a lower boiling point so they evaporate easily and float in the air. Essential oils of other plants have been used as medicines for thousands of years. They have been overlooked because they are much subtler than the cannabinoids and their effects were overshadowed. Nevertheless they may have many qualities useful for aromatherapy. In the next few years they will be isolated and tested for their efficacy. I hope to be a subject in the experiments, which are unplanned at this time as far as I know.

As people are given more choice and become more knowledgeable about marijuana's varied qualities and the different mental and physical effects, breeders will be under increasing pressure to develop varieties that produce specific highs or therapeutic effects. As part of this momentum for clearer, more specific highs, breeders will also be encouraged to select for the other psychoactive aromatic essential oils.

Ripening Time

When outdoor growers first tried to grow seeds from tropical varieties that were included in the imports, the plants often died of cold before they started flowering or were harvested when the flowers were still young. The big breakthrough came when trekkers brought back the higher latitude Indicas and the subgroup Afghanis. These 30-degree latitude plants flowered in September and October, much earlier than the Sativas. They provided

Masaya's 27 mental states of high

Giggly	Energetic	Physical
Munchies	Couch Lock	Cerebral
Euphoric	Stoney	Heavy
Trippy	Head-Body	Active
Strong	Mellow	Sleepy
Cheerful	Alert	Narcotic
Smooth	Clear	Relaxing
Uplifting	Creepy	Psychedelic
Eyedroop	Visual	Creative

stock to work with and were used to shorten ripening time in three of the four progenitor varieties. As more Indica landraces became available to breeders, they were reintroduced to Sativa backcrosses to shorten ripening time.

In the future, breeders will take many roads to adapt their plants to local conditions. All along the coast of North America, from southern California to the lower Canadian coast, breeders are adapting varieties to local conditions. They choose plants that ripen early, before the fog, rains, search crews or robbers get them. I expect plants that are harvestable in late August to become common in the next few years.

Indoor varieties have branched off from their outdoor siblings. Plants are being developed that will ripen faster and faster. The difference between a 70-day and a 60-day flowering cycle can be as much as a crop per year. The trend is likely to continue. Many gardeners claim to have a very early ripening plant. However, when these claims have been investigated, it was found that the flowers were going to be harvested before they were ripe. Still, I expect to see 45-day plants within a few years.

Another possibility is developing plants that automatically flower; that is, plants that flower without depend-

Top: This mostly Sativa hybrid has shorter internodes, more foliage and more bud sites than a purebred Sativa. It was grown in a greenhouse that dispersed light to lower branches and inner sections needed for a Sativa to grow properly.
Bottom: This is Alien Trainwreck. Without training, the plant grows into a rounded bush with long colas (spikes of buds). The highest colas are only four feet high which makes it suitable for home gardens and indoor growing. This plant would be a good candidate for indoor gardens where the plant numbers are limited and each plant must be a heavy yielder.

ing on a light regimen as their trigger. Equatorial plants use other indicators, perhaps size and age, to trigger flowering. Perhaps we will find a quirky Sativa that likes to flower early and has a self-trigger. All we need is one plant to change the world's genetics.

This landrace Moroccan variety, common in the Rif Mountains of North Africa, grows only a single stem. The plants are grown very close together. However, when plants were spaced so that they had room to branch, they kept the single-stem morphology. This variety could be used in a breeding program to develop plants especially adapted to sea of green gardens. The variety is weak but its genetics could be used in a breeding program. Single stem plants are the most efficient for the sea of green method.

This strange hybrid grew an almost cylindrical top branch section resulting from short branches. The lower branches stretched out and grew prostrate along the ground.

Growth Pattern

Grow a pure Sativa, even a short season variety, and you will see a graceful specimen with long stems between each pair of branches. It will have thin, long-fingered leaves that almost seem to weep. It will grow 8 to 15 feet tall and will have the stature of a graceful Christmas tree. It's certainly beautiful to look at, but is not the most productive plant.

Indica plants grow in several patterns. Some are rounded and bushy, others are asymmetrical and still others look like compact Sativas. These varieties tame the Sativas and bulk them out. Indicas have thicker, heavier buds and the characteristic is expressed in hybrids with Sativas.

After thirty years of breeding, marijuana plants come in many sizes and growth patterns. There are large plants, small ones, plants that are sparingly branched and bushy ones. Some produce small buds while others grow a few large buds and others produce lots of large buds.

Varieties have also been acclimated to thousands of different microclimates by millions of growers. Plants have been bred to thrive in particular environments, such as hot or cold environments, or wet and dry conditions. Growers in humid areas and indoor growers have created mold resistant strains. The genetics will eventually be transferred to the commercial market, sometimes internationally, but probably more often on a local basis. (As in: "Here are some seeds my brother's friend grew from two dynamite plants last year.")

What's in the future? To a great extent, breeding will be driven by several considerations. First and foremost, the law has many ramifications. Communities in states with medical marijuana laws have enacted various restrictions limiting patient's rights to cultivate. There are basically three kinds of laws: plant number limits, space limits or total light wattage limits. Some laws use a combination of these factors to arrive at their regulations.

Each of these laws calls for a different strategy. If plant number is the limiting factor, growers will want to grow large, high yielding specimens, even indoors. If space is the limiting factor and plant numbers aren't significant, growers will opt for smaller, fast growing, single-stem plants. Each plant uses a small portion of the canopy, so it doesn't have to grow very much. The canopy gets covered with vegetation in a very short time, so the plants can be forced to flower quickly. Moroccan plants grow single stems and could be used in a breeding program.

When the total wattage is limited growers will also choose fast growing plants suitable for sea of green systems. Growers should also consider the plants' light intensity requirements. Plants that require less light for fast growth can be spread over a larger area to maximize yield.

The "California Creeper" is a plant that grows prostrate to the ground. A single plant can cover an area as large as 100 square feet (approximately 10 square meters). This plant's unique characteristics and other plants with similar traits could revolutionize how marijuana is grown both indoors and out. Imagine a shelf or cliff with branches trailing down. The buds grow in spikes that look like eight-inch candles. This year a plant with similar characteristics was discovered in a garden in Oregon. Prostrate plants are probably growing in many gardens throughout North America and Europe.

Plants with leaves that don't look like cannabis, either in color or pattern, could also be valuable to some growers. If the plant isn't recognized, then it isn't in jeopardy. Breeding a leaf that has more of a maple leaf shape or which has variegated colors such as green and white or green and purple might camouflage a plant, especially if it is an unusual shape such as a bushy mound, a large single stem, or prostrate.

Other Breeding Goals

Breeders are always looking for new innovative plants. When the percentage of leaf to flower is decreased, potency goes up because the flower area contains more glands than the leaves. Plants with low leaf-to-flower ratio are always considered desirable.

Manicuring is a chore. If a plant were bred to drop its leaves at bud maturity, it would save a lot of tedious labor spent manicuring. Occasionally a Sativa exhibits this characteristic, but I don't know any breeding programs considering this.

Have you ever noticed that both indoors and out, some buds on a plant are mature while others are still ripening? Wouldn't it be great if the entire plant ripened at the same time? This is still another convenience that breeders could aim for—a plant that matures all at once.

In the book *The Botany of Desire*, Michael Pollan wrote that prohibition has been very good to cannabis. Millions of people are growing it and it has colonized a new environment, the indoor grow room. The scarcity of good seed or clones has forced people into home breeding. As a result instead of a few crosses or experiments there are thousands of ongoing concurrent breeding programs that are all aimed at producing perfect matches between genetics and environment. We can look forward to some great advances in the next few years as the new strains become commercially available.

FRESH LEAVES

One day when Oden was manicuring some fresh bud he noticed how much more hash was sticking to his fingers as compared with when he manicured dry weed. He found that the wet resin was much tackier and built up faster on his hands. His inquiring mind wondered whether he could make hash with fresh, just-picked material. This was of some importance to him because leaf is a by-product of bud production and he grew bud for the medical dispensaries in California.

FRESH HASH
makes wonderful stash

VARIETIES DIFFER in the ratio of leaf to bud and the potency of the leaf. Leaf with many glands on it yields more hash, but it won't necessarily be stronger than less glandular leaf. Bud yields a lot more hash than leaf but it is usually uneconomical to use. Leaf can contain quite a bit of THC while still being inexpensive and, using Oden's method, the quality of the hash does not differ much.

You can't rub the fresh leaf on a simple 110-thread kief screen the way you can with dry leaf because the resin will clog it up. Instead Oden developed his own water method for extracting resin from leaf. The hash-making technique Oden refined works very well and takes an hour or less to complete. In this demonstration he started with a kilogram of mixed green marijuana leaf. However, it isn't unusual to process five kilograms at a time using the same equipment.

Before starting, the bud is examined to get an idea of the density of the crystals. He will repeat this examination after 15 minutes of beating and then again after another 15 minutes to make sure that most of the glands have separated from the vegetative material.

His first step was to chop the fresh or frozen leaf into pieces no larger than a half inch square. When he tried using un-chopped leaf, it balled around the mixer tines later in the process.

"His inquiring mind wondered whether he could make hash with fresh, just-picked material."

"I chopped it finer so it mixes in the water without balling. I place the chopped leaf in a 30-gallon waste can that has not been used for other purposes. It's one of a pair of matching containers. Ten pounds of leaf fills the container about one-third of a standard trash container's height. Then I add ice cubes to double that height. I add cold water to float the ice, which increases the height of the grass-ice by about half again. At the end, I figure, by volume, one third each of grass, ice and water.

"I use concrete mixing tines attached to a powerful 1/2-inch drill set at slow speed to agitate the mix for about 15 minutes. Neither the leaf nor the ice should be crushed. The leaf shouldn't be beaten or damaged too much. I just want to knock the glands off. After 15 minutes I check the crystal content of the leaf. Most of the time I get back to agitating. I only finish when the great majority of crystals has been knocked off. The next step is to separate the glands from the leaf that's been beaten into pulp. I use a spaghetti strainer to pour the water-gland solution into the

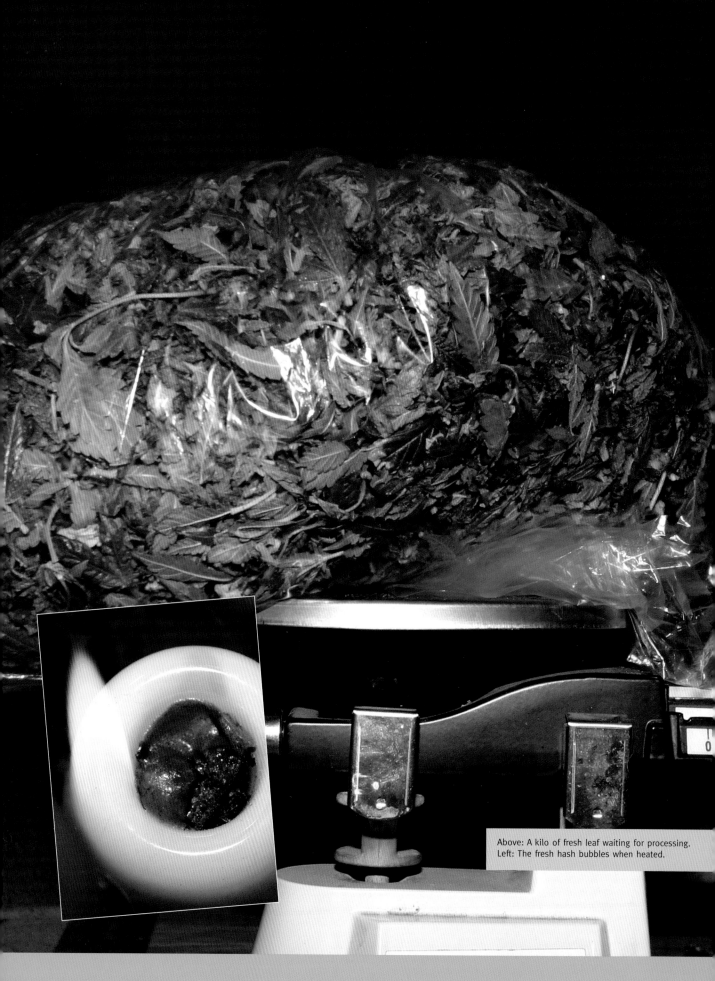

Above: A kilo of fresh leaf waiting for processing.
Left: The fresh hash bubbles when heated.

Top: The grass is diced into pieces no larger than a half-inch. Inset: Close-up of the miracle of water hash.

other matched container. A 30-gallon container of water is pretty heavy, so I use a one-gallon container to move the water-pulp solution. Once the can is partly drained I might lift it with the help of a friend. I use the pulp I recover for cooking. I strain all the water through the sieve. Only the pulpy leaf is left. Then I rinse the pulp with a small amount of water to remove any remaining crystals. I run the water through a second filter. It's a wood framed 16"x 20" 110-count silkscreen with 90-micron openings. To condition it each time for use, wet it on each side and then rub your hands on the backside. If the

screen is used before it's pre-conditioned, water will bead up and run off it.

"The water is poured through the screen. It leaves a residue of calyxes, leaf bits and other plant material. This pulp is then rinsed on the screen with

> "Bud yields a lot more hash than leaf but it is usually uneconomical to use."

a small amount of water while being agitated with a Medical Cannabis Authorization Card. This is added to the pulp to be used later. I don't use my hands because their heat will melt the resins and they'll stick to the threads, ruining the screen. Scrubbing with rubbing alcohol and then rinsing can salvage it, but it's a tedious task.

"Now it's time to filter the glands from the water. I thoroughly rinse out the empty container and make sure it is 100% free of all debris, leaf, calyxes, hairs or any other residue. I do this in the shower for convenience.

The chopped grass is tossed into the processing container.

Ice and water are added to the processor.

The cement mixer tine. The grass is agitated for 15 to 30 minutes on slow speed using a powerful drill.

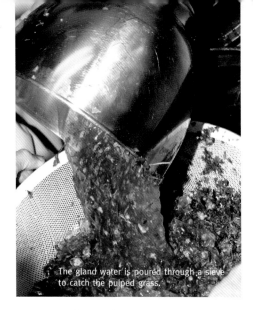
The gland water is poured through a sieve to catch the pulped grass.

The gland water is filtered through a silk screen sieve to catch residue and debris.

The debris is collected with a Marijuana Medical Card and added to the pulped grass.

"I designed a tool for the next step to get around the old drain and wait method. That is to let all the glands separate from the water mix and drift to the bottom of the barrel. This takes hours. Most of the water is drained and then the residue (the glands) is collected from the remaining water using coffee filters.

"I use a stocking made from coarse silk cloth with smaller openings as the final filter. It allows about one-fifth, 7 out of 35 grams, to pass through. The lower grade smaller glands degrade the quality of the hash but aren't usually filtered out using other water hash methods. Only the larger crystals remain in the special sock."

Oden himself sewed this secret formula stocking with traditional seam to custom fit snugly over the top of the barrel. He experimented with many grades of silk until he found exactly the right one. This secret, like the formula for red glass in the film *"Heart of Glass,"* will die with Oden. Hopefully, while he is alive, he will reproduce many examples of his work, so his legacy will continue for many generations—a Stradivarius of glands.

"The stocking covers the barrel rim and quickly tapers to a toe at the very bottom. It's longer than the trash can so the toe sits on the bottom. It was designed this way because having long sides allows the glands to sit flat on the bottom even when water is poured from the other container."

Once again he used a one-gallon pitcher to move the water into the stocking filter. For convenience a larger container or a pump can be used. As the water flows into the stocking it drains mostly into the surrounding container. Most of the water and lower quality glands pass through. The stocking contains water and the larger high quality glands.

Smoking a joint, a necessary step according to Oden, allows the glands within the stocking to settle to the toe at its bottom. Lifting it out of the water all at once would plug the stocking's tiny holes. Instead, raising the stocking slowly from the container puts gentle pressure on the crystals to drift down. By hoisting the stocking 10 inches above the water level the glands

"Leaf can contain quite a bit of THC while still being inexpensive..."

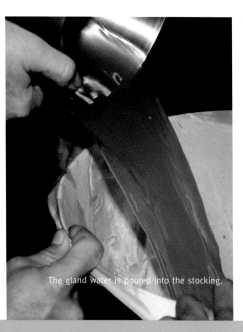
The gland water is poured into the stocking.

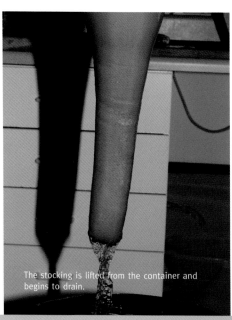
The stocking is lifted from the container and begins to drain.

After several dunkings and rinses most of the water has drained from the stocking, leaving the hash.

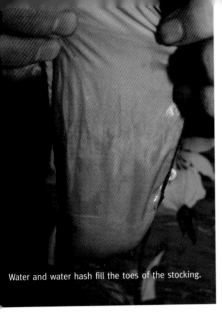

Water and water hash fill the toes of the stocking.

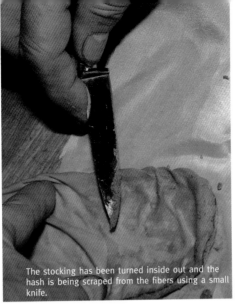

The stocking has been turned inside out and the hash is being scraped from the fibers using a small knife.

The hash ball, wrapped in silk cloth, is being wrapped in a cloth towel.

attached to the side fall away. Continuing this process a few more times, raising the stocking higher each time, keeps the pressure low so the glands drift down rather than push against the holes. Eventually they gather in a big ball at the toe as the water drains from the stocking and it can be comfortably held with one hand.

In a few minutes the loose water and lower quality smaller glands drain out, leaving only the larger glands. Oden dipped the stocking one more time and then raised it. This allowed residual glands to drift down from the sides. He held the tip of the stocking gently in paper towels. He didn't squeeze. The towels wicked the water out.

Oden removed the ball from the stocking by turning it inside out. Then using the same medical card he scraped the stocking for any clinging resin and

added it to the ball. He wrapped the ball in a small piece of silk cloth made from the same material as the stocking, wrapped that in paper towels, then

> "Before starting, the bud is examined to get an idea of the density of the crystals."

wrapped that in a cloth towel and placed it on the floor. Using a 220 lb., 50-year-old press he then heeled the ball. Water still in the hash ball was pushed out and absorbed by the towels. The hash was almost ready to test.

Before being smoked it needed some hand kneading to release the final bit of moisture. Oden kneaded it and worked it into shape after shape from rectangle to log to ball. Finally he stretched it into

a thick log and tore it open so we could view the raw glands. The hash was ready. We took a good look at it and realized we had witnessed a miracle. Was this a pieta or a temptation? We weighed the hash at 7.13 grams.

Oden insisted on testing the hash. He put it in his pipe and held fire to it. It bubbled and vaporized before it finally yielded some ash. The vapor had more of an essence than a taste and it was very potent. The water hash stripped away the extraneous vegetative material and delivered only the high.

The next day Oden repeated the stocking treatment on the rinsed water and harvested another 3.5 grams. This hash was also excellent but it was not the extremely high quality of the first batch and it didn't bubble.

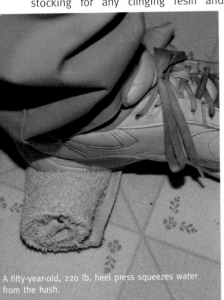

A fifty-year-old, 220 lb. heel press squeezes water from the hash.

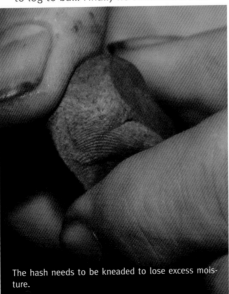

The hash needs to be kneaded to lose excess moisture.

A rectangular shape formed during the kneading process.

MAKING

Just before Reagan became president, the U.S. Supreme Court ruled that living organisms modified through the use of genetic engineering were patentable. The incoming president left the field unregulated, permitting corporations to experiment with monster creations in the environment. This laissez-faire government policy has given corporations the go-ahead to produce genetically modified food products grown on plants with genes stolen from animals and other organisms.

HASHIMALS
fun on the farm

AS A RESULT OF GENETIC engineering, farmers all over North America are battling corporations such as Monsanto just for the right to continue to farm naturally. Consumers are facing Hobson's choices. Almost all soy grown in North America is genetically engineered. It makes it hard to eat healthy.

For this reason I was concerned when I heard that a medical marijuana provider was involved in a similar activity. Some friends mentioned that Oden was at a party and was demonstrating how his recently created animals were able to do "tricks." Further, they had been developed using only plant genetics.

I called Oden, and he confirmed that he had indeed been acting as an "intelligent creator" and was planning on developing new creatures in the next few days. He invited me over to observe the delicate operation.

Upon entering the structure located in an old industrial section of San Francisco, I would never have suspected it to be a laboratory where new life forms are developed on a regular basis. It was designed to look like a loft apartment, and the specially designed equipment could have been mistaken for household items. I thought to myself that this was truly an ingenious way of keeping the research center discreet and under the radar.

> **"He assured me that they were harmless, playful creatures. "**

Oden guided me to the lab bench cleverly disguised as a kitchen table. Getting to the point, I asked him if it was true that he had created animals using plant material. He said that he had. A wry

Close-up of a hash shark. Rather than taking a bite out of you, it is more likely that its tail will be clipped, then a fin, then...

Below: The folded log is the starting point of the artistic process. Inset: The piece of water hash shortly after being made. It still contains a lot of water.

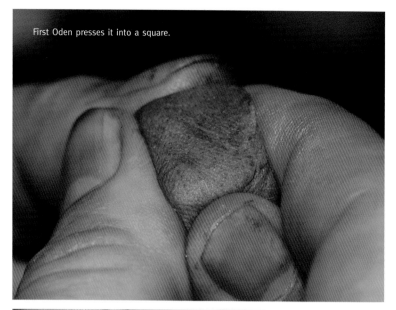
First Oden presses it into a square.

Then he rolls it into a ball. It still contains a lot of water and "sweats" when rolled around.

The paperclip is used to smooth out the sides.

smile, almost a smirk, escaped from the tiniest muscle in his lips and quickly spread to the other 25 muscles in his face.

He assured me that they were harmless, playful creatures. He was able to conceive them, he told me, but the creatures were not able to reproduce by themselves, so there has been no proliferation problem. "In fact," he mentioned, "I have given several of these as pets to friends, but all of them have disappeared into the vapor."

Then he said the words I wanted to hear, "Would you like to see my zoo?" I quickly affirmed my interest. Surprisingly, he opened a temperature controlled freezer unit. I thought, "The animals are kept in suspended animation at cold temperature, much like insects."

He must have read my mind because he said, "They only become pliable and lively when they reach room temperature." He gently removed the little golden objects from a zip-type plastic bag. They came tumbling out onto a soft towel.

I thought my hearing must be worse than I imagined. These aren't animals, they're hashimals. And of course they're made of plant material. What else would they be made of? Last time I looked, hash was a plant product.

Then he asked if I would like to watch him create a hashimal. "I sure would," I said.

Oden said that we should start with a freshly made piece of hash. He happened to have some on hand, so he was able to demonstrate his artistry. He started by taking an oval lump of golden water hash that he finished making just a few minutes earlier.

The hash was very soft and blond. It was wet to the touch and still contained a lot of water from the refining

Trainwreck Octo is so lubricated, he's leaking.

Top: Modern micro-technology using a pin helps the fish develop rays and other features. Inset: Full-body view of the newest creature, the Golden Sun-leaf fish.

process. He placed it on a silk cloth, folded the cloth over it, and folded a towel over that. Then he pressed his palm on the towel, letting his weight act as a vise to press the water from the hash. The water passed through the silk cloth and was absorbed by the towel.

> **"He was able to conceive them, he told me, but the creatures were not able to reproduce by themselves, so there has been no proliferation problem."**

He used a knife to gently scrape the pressed material sticking to the silk. He lifted the scraping from the knife and pressed it into a solid piece. Then he used the sticky mass to collect hash still on the cloth. It was drier, but still very moist. He pressed it into a square and then started working on the sculpture.

He rolled it into a ball in the palms of his hands using a circular motion. As he rolled it, the surface sweated water. The

surface became smooth and went from a matte finish to shiny. Then, instead of rolling his palms circularly, he moved them back and forth. The ball soon became a sweating log.

It looked a lot like he was working with clay. It was pliable and easy to mold and shape. Just like clay, some of it stuck to the skin and had to be scraped off.

Placing the fate of his creation in his hands, he folded the log over and shaped it into a rectangle. Then, using an unbent paper clip, he smoothed out the surface to an even layer. Next he started pressing the hash, making it thinner and giving the top a rounded shape. The extruded and pressed material miraculously formed side fins. The rounded back of the dorsal fin took shape.

The fish was evolving from a lump of "clay." Next, the fine detail showed the perfection of intelligent creation. Oden started to give his creation individuality. Using a pin, he developed a spinal cord with bones attached that held the fins in place. Picking up a few tiny pieces of primal matter, he rolled and flattened them and attached them to the unsighted creature, to give it at least a set of eyes. Voilà! Another creature had evolved.

Top: The Sun-leaf fish is very friendly. Here it's hanging out with a human "friend."
Below: An Afghani loco-bird.

"I thought my hearing must be worse than I imagined. These aren't animals, they're hash-imals."

Here it was right before my eyes. Oden had taken plant material and, using the alchemy of modern science and technology, had made a golden sun-leaf fish. My fears were relieved because I knew that it had the likelihood of survival of a Chips-Ahoy® cookie at a kid's birthday party. No matter how many of these creatures come into being, they will be captured and, like salmon, smoked.

Oden has many of his creations in his exotic aquarium. There they bask in cool darkness and slowly lose their water and ripen. Little do they know that, as they grow older and lose weight, the day of their extinction grows near. Just as a human created these new forms, their existence will cease in a wisp of vapor and a little ash.

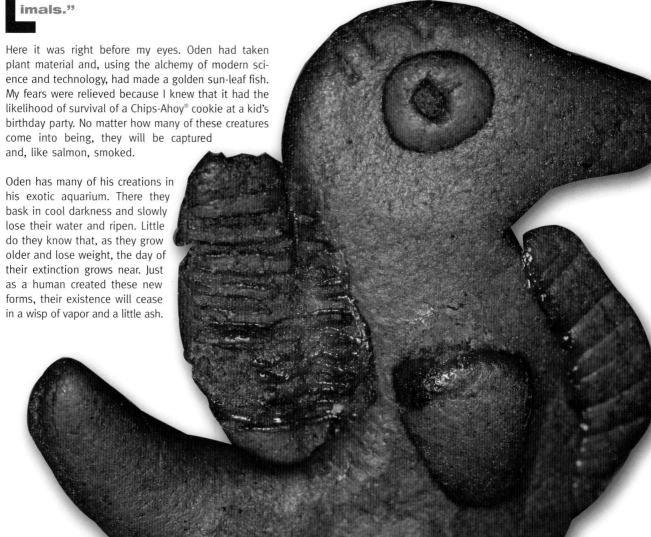